# SERIAL KILLERS

# SERIAL KILLERS

## WILLIAM MURRAY

canary press

Barnes & Noble
122 Fifth Avenue
New York, NY  10011

ISBN: 978-0-7607-9658-0

Printed and bound in Singapore

10 9 8 7 6 5 4 3 2

Cover and internal design: Anthony Prudente on behalf of Omnipress Limited
Images: courtesy of Getty, Corbis, PA Photos, Reuters, Topfoto, iStockphoto and Fotolia

# INTRODUCTION

In the early 1980s the USA was in the grip of an epidemic of a particular type of murder. The perpetrators targeted certain groups of people and followed a set pattern to kill multiple times. The FBI, including Robert Ressler, one of the best known investigators of these killings, began to call them serial killers. Films, books and TV cop shows popularised the term and it found an immediate resonance in the public imagination. The shocking and terrible nature of these crimes caused levels of fear and panic out of all proportion to the actual numbers of killings. With a serial killer on the loose, nobody felt safe.

Unlike the majority of murderers, serial killers don't know their victims prior to the attacks. Their motive is purely one of personal gratification, which is generally sexual in nature. It made the job of catching them extremely difficult and led law enforcement agencies in America, and subsequently in other parts of the world, to develop new investigative methods. The FBI began a systematic study of serial killers, starting with a definition of what they were dealing with. Serial killers, according to the FBI, commit three or more murders in separate attacks in different locations, usually with a cooling off period between each killing, which can be a matter of weeks, months or even years.

In this book the cases of 36 different serial killers are examined. Although each is distinctive, certain similarities between many of them soon become apparent. Recognising and describing the phenomenon is, of course, not the same as understanding it. Perhaps these crimes are so appalling they are beyond any form of understanding, but, as the FBI have found out, the more you know about serial killers, the more effectively they can be stopped.

Robert Ressler was one of the pioneers of the use psychological profiling. Patterns of similar behaviour, often beginning in childhood, were recorded for a number of serial killers even though they operated in completely different ways. Many experienced some form of abuse or trauma in their early childhood, which developed into psychosis later in life. The first signs of this psychosis could be seen in a child's abnormal behaviour, expressed as, for example, an excessive cruelty to animals or acts of arson. The vast majority of children exhibiting these traits don't go on to kill anyone, but recognising they exist in serial killers can be used to narrow down a field of potential suspects in an investigation.

There are a number of other common traits, which crop up again and again in the serial killers detailed in this book. As well as fulfilling perverse sexual fantasies, many serial killers also need to be in control of their victims. They feel no empathy with the people they kill and no sense of remorse for what they have done. Once a serial killer has started killing and has established a particular pattern of behaviour, known as their modus operandi, the interval between attacks usually gets shorter and the attacks become increasingly violent. It is as if the thrill of each successive attack wears off more quickly the more times a serial killer repeats the pattern.

Another common feature is for a serial killer to take something from the victim as a souvenir, allowing them to relive the initial thrill of the attack over and over again. The killer usually becomes more confident in his ability to get away with murder as the number of victims mounts and will often contact the police and news media to gloat over the notoriety they have achieved. And they very rarely stop killing once they have started, until they are caught or killed.

Serial killers can compartmentalise their crimes, separating them from the rest of their lives. Between killings they often appear to be relatively normal, rarely acting like the madmen we might expect them to be. It is not unusual for a serial killer to be married and to hold down a steady job. When they are caught, their neighbours often express shock and disbelief after the apparently normal person they knew has been exposed as a monster. This, together with the terrible nature of the crimes, is one of the most chilling aspects of the phenomenon. A serial killer could be living next door to any one of us.

# CONTENTS

CONVICTED MURDERS **1**

SUSPECTED MURDERS **15**

A.K.A. THE RUGELEY POISONER

METHOD STRYCHNINE POISONING

# WILLIAM PALMER

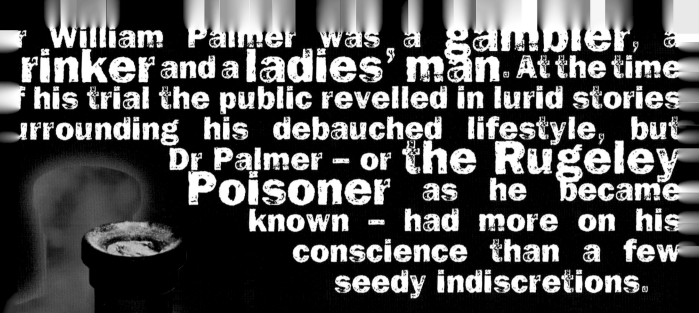

Dr William Palmer was a gambler, a drinker and a ladies' man. At the time of his trial the public revelled in lurid stories surrounding his debauched lifestyle, but Dr Palmer – or the Rugeley Poisoner as he became known – had more on his conscience than a few seedy indiscretions.

In one of the most sensational trials of 19th century Britain, Dr William Palmer, of Rugeley in Staffordshire, was found guilty of murdering John Parsons Cook by poisoning him with strychnine, the first such conviction in British legal history. After Palmer's arrest, the notoriety of the case led to an Act of Parliament, later known as the Palmer Act, passed to allow the trial to be transferred from Staffordshire to the Old Bailey in London.

The public were fascinated by details of Palmer's debauched lifestyle that were revealed in newspapers of the day. Salacious tales of compulsive womanizing and excessive gambling shocked conservative Victorian society and ultimately served to hasten Palmer's conviction for Cook's murder. But there are many who believe his trial represents a travesty of justice and that Palmer was found guilty more for his notorious reputation than by the evidence presented by his prosecutors. Some believed that a 'show trial' was engineered by the British government to distract public attention from the perilous state of the country at the time. But could the publicity surrounding the immoral misdeeds of one man, however scandalous, really be expected to save an unpopular government?

Controversy had followed Palmer for decades prior to his arrest. Friends, patients and even his immediate family continued to die with alarming frequency, and more often than not Palmer stood to gain from their deaths. He was born into a respectable middle-class family and trained as a doctor in London and at Stafford Infirmary, where rumours surrounding his drinking and gambling first began. He is thought to have shown an unusual, and not entirely healthy, interest in the poisons kept in the dispensary, although it is worth noting that many poisons were widely used in conventional

The first mysterious death occurred in 1846, shortly after Palmer had qualified as a doctor and set up practice in Rugeley. On a cold and wet October night Palmer arranged to meet George Abley, a plumber, in a local pub. As was Palmer's habit, he made a bet with Abley concerning the plumber's ability to drink copious amounts of brandy. Abley won the bet, but became violently ill and left the pub shortly afterwards. Some hours later he was found dead in the stables outside. The Staffordshire coroner recorded a verdict of death by natural causes. Abley was suffering from tuberculosis and could have died from this, exacerbated by the adverse weather conditions and by alcohol poisoning. Nevertheless, rumours about his death would not be quashed and gossip was rife surrounding the exact nature of Palmer's relationship with Abley's wife, who was a regular patient of the 'good doctor'.

A year later Palmer married the beautiful and fascinating Anne Thornton (Annie), the daughter of a well-heeled family who owned a number of properties in the Rugeley area. Mary Thornton, Annie's mother, took an instant dislike to Palmer – possibly because she'd been party to local gossip – but in January 1849, Mary became ill and, despite her reservations, moved into her son-in-law's house. Within only a few weeks, Mary died and although she had been suffering from the effects of years of alcohol abuse,

# COMPULSIVE WOMANIZING & EXCESSIVE GAMBLING

the coincidental timing of her death added fuel to the fire. Palmer probably expected his wife to benefit substantially from her mother's will but, if he did, he was wrong. Mary Thornton didn't leave any of her portfolio of properties to Annie. Perhaps Palmer had underestimated his mother-in-law.

Over the next six years an unusual number of Palmer's patients and creditors died shortly after leaving his company. During the same period his wife gave birth to five children, but only one survived for more than a few months. In September 1854, Annie also became ill and was diagnosed, by another doctor,

as suffering from cholera. She died a few days later. After Annie's death it transpired that Palmer had taken out a large life insurance policy on her only weeks before she fell ill, and he had only paid the first instalment by the time of her death. There is no direct evidence to link Palmer to the death of his wife, but it is hardly surprising that some people jumped to certain conclusions. A year later Palmer's brother also died shortly after Palmer had taken out a policy on him. This time the insurance company refused to pay out.

In November 1855 Palmer committed the crime that sealed his fate forever. He accompanied his friend and fellow gambler John Parsons Cook to a race meeting in Shrewsbury. Cook got lucky, winning £3,000, an enormous amount of money for the time. Palmer, as usual, lost heavily. At a dinner to celebrate his big win Cook began to feel unwell and returned to Rugeley with Palmer, taking up residence at the Talbot Inn. Cook never checked out. Within days of his death Palmer went to London to collect Cook's winnings. A postmortem and inquest were held at the insistence of Cook's stepfather, and a verdict of wilful murder was returned. Palmer was found to have bought strychnine just days before Cook's death and was arrested. The official reason for transferring the trial to the Old Bailey was because it was thought a Staffordshire jury would be prejudiced by local hearsay. Even at the time some believed the transfer had more to do with focusing public attention on Palmer's debauched

dealings rather than the government's on-going problems. A guilty verdict was reached and Palmer was sentenced to death. He was returned to Stafford Prison where, at 8am on 14 June 1856, over 30,000 people flocked to see him hanged by the neck.

It is impossible to say, over 150 years after the events, whether Palmer was definitely guilty of any or all of the murders for which he stood accused. It is certainly true that he was an entirely self-involved and ruthless man who showed absolutely no concern for anyone else, neither his friends and family nor the patients whose care had been entrusted to him. William Palmer had the mentality of a serial killer, which is what has led to him being dubbed the Prince of Poisoners and has seen him go down in history as a prototype for the killer-doctors who would follow, including the infamous Harold Shipman.

ABOVE: The poisoning case at Rugeley, the trial of William Palmer in the central criminal court.
OPPOSITE PAGE: Dr William Palmer, 1856.

# 30,000 PEOPLE FLOCKED TO SEE WILLIAM PALMER HANGED BY THE NECK

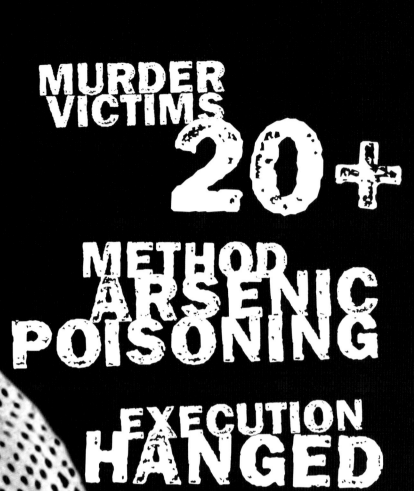

MURDER VICTIMS 20+

METHOD ARSENIC POISONING

EXECUTION HANGED

MARY ANN COTTON

# Mary Ann Cotton murdered multiple husbands, lovers and even her own children. People around her were dropping like flies, but when one after another succumbed to mysterious 'intestinal disorders' no-one raised an eyebrow. Did she kill out of poverty or for pleasure?

The female serial killer is a rare phenomenon. Broadly speaking they can mostly be divided into two types: the Angel of Death and the Black Widow. The Angel of Death is typically a nurse who takes it upon herself to relieve the suffering of her patients by killing them, often by administering a lethal dose of a drug the patient is already taking. The Black Widow specializes in murdering husbands and lovers, using her charms to lure unsuspecting men into her trap. Mary Ann Cotton falls into this latter category, killing three of her four husbands and one of her many lovers. But she didn't stop there. Over a 20-year period she had 12 children, and all but one died in infancy of 'gastric fever'. Her stepchildren were not safe either, most of them dying in a similar fashion – as did her own mother and a number of other relatives. The symptoms of arsenic poisoning are similar to those of gastric fever, and arsenic was freely available in those days as it was mainly used to kill household pests.

Mary was born in Sunderland, in north-east England, in 1832. Her father was a coal miner and a harsh disciplinarian. He was killed after he fell down a mine shaft at the pit where he worked when Mary was eight. The family sank into poverty and Mary would retain a fear of becoming destitute for the rest of her life. This hardly excuses her subsequent crimes, but it does provide a motivation for them as they all revolved around money. Her mother remarried, easing the family's money worries, but Mary didn't get on with her stepfather. She moved out of the family home when she was sixteen to become a nurse. At twenty she married her first husband, William Mowbray, and moved to Plymouth, in Devon. The couple had five children there, but four died in infancy from what doctors called intestinal disorders. On moving back north Mary had three more children, each succumbing to something similar. They would be quickly followed by their father. Mary showed little emotion. She collected the payout on Mowbray's life insurance and moved on.

The next victim was George Ward, who she married in 1865. He lasted a little over a year before developing stomach trouble and dying. His doctor expressed surprise at the speed of his death, but no investigation took place and Mary collected the money from another life insurance policy. The lives of poor people were cheap in those days and doctors were busy.

James Robinson, Mary's third husband, was more cautious than the previous two. After his children began to die he started to suspect all was not right. Mary tried to talk him into taking out a life insurance policy, but he wasn't having it and threw her out of his house. She promptly moved in with the more gullible Frederick Cotton and, with terrible inevitability, his children began to die. The couple entered into a bigamous marriage, as Mary was still married to Robinson. Needless to say, not long after taking out life insurance, Cotton began to show the same symptoms as all the others and died shortly afterwards.

The next on the list was Joseph Nattrass, who moved into Mary's house not long after Frederick Cotton had been buried. Mary got a job as a nurse to John Quick-Manning and an affair began. She became pregnant for the twelfth time with Quick-Manning's child and decided he was going to be her next husband. Nattrass's and Cotton's three surviving sons were getting in the way of her plans, but Mary wasn't going to let them put a stop to her latest scheme. Soon only one child was left, Charles Cotton, with Nattrass and the two other boys going the way of all the others. The death of Charles, the last impediment to her marriage to Quick-Manning, would be her downfall. A local magistrate saw him a few days before he died and thought he looked to be in perfect health. On hearing of the boy's death, he went to the police and

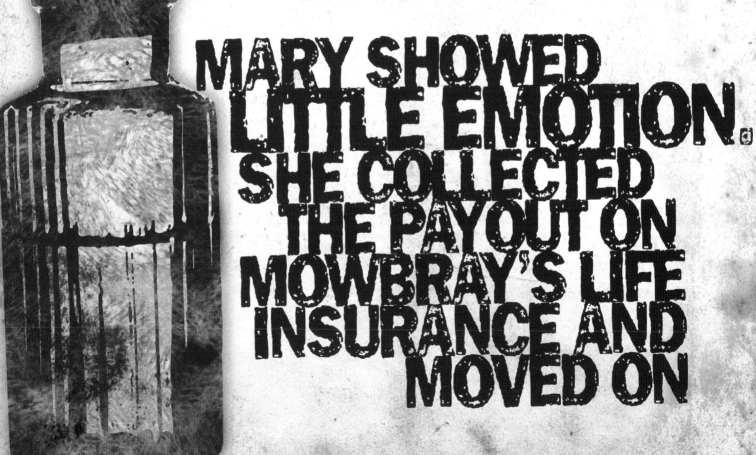

MARY SHOWED LITTLE EMOTION. SHE COLLECTED THE PAYOUT ON MOWBRAY'S LIFE INSURANCE AND MOVED ON

an inquiry began. The boy was found to have been poisoned with arsenic and Mary was arrested for his murder.

It seems incredible now for a string of deaths from such similar causes to go unnoticed for so long. But in the 19th century death from what would now be considered preventable causes was a common occurrence, particularly among the young and the poor. Mary may even have been the object of pity among the people who knew her, as her husband and children had all died in such quick succession. Perhaps the money she collected from all the different insurance policies should have raised more eyebrows than it apparently did. The insurance companies themselves could have demanded inquiries into any of the deaths, but they didn't. Mary changed her surname every time she got married, so they might not have realized it was the same person collecting the money on so many different people.

Mary was put on trial for the murder of Charles Cotton. It lasted a few weeks and, while it was going on, investigative journalists uncovered details of the deaths of her previous husbands and children. Not being constrained by the laws of libel and contempt of court, as the press are now, lurid stories about Mary were published before the trial had finished. The prosecution attempted to introduce these revelations into the case, but the trial judge would not allow it. She was found guilty of murder by arsenic poisoning and was sentenced to death. Petitions attempting to commute the sentence to life imprisonment failed, and she was hanged at Durham County Jail on 24 March 1873. The hangman botched the job. He misjudged the length of rope needed to do it properly and, instead of dying instantly from a broken neck, Mary was left to swing at the end of the rope, slowly strangling to death.

**MURDER VICTIMS**
**5**

**METHOD**
**THROAT CUT**
**BODY MUTILATED**

# JACK THE RIPPER

# The individual known as Jack the Ripper has gone down in history as the most infamous serial killer of all time. The frenzied attacks committed in his name ignited the public's imagination and spawned countless articles, novels and films. Despite our collective obsession with his crimes, one question still remains – who the devil was he?

Whitechapel, in the East End of London, was a place of grinding poverty in the late 19th century. Drunkenness and prostitution were rife and violent crime a part of everyday life. Even so, the Whitechapel Murders, beginning in August 1888, terrorized the area and the nation. It quickly became apparent that a maniac was on the loose, a prototype serial killer. The attacks followed a pattern: the victims were all prostitutes, the method of killing was the same – although it became progressively more violent and gruesome – and the only apparent motive was sexual. Letters purportedly from the killer were sent to the police investigating the murders, most were hoaxes by journalists attempting to sensationalize the case even further. Others were not so easily dismissed. They taunted the police and gave details of the crimes.

They also provided a name for the killer – Jack the Ripper.

The first victim was Mary Ann Nichols. She was found lying in a stable doorway on Bucks Row in the early hours of Friday 31 August. Her throat had been cut down to the bone and her stomach slashed, exposing her intestines. The savagery of the attack attracted attention, even though the murder of prostitutes in the East End at that time was an all too common occurrence. A week later, on Saturday 8 September, Annie Chapman's body was found in the backyard of a barber's shop in Hanbury Street, not far from where Mary Ann had been killed. The knife wounds were similar, but, this time, her intestines had been pulled out

and her uterus cut out and taken away. The murder had obviously been committed by the same killer. A doctor who examined the bodies said the murderer showed a knowledge of anatomy and was skilled in the use of a knife. Could the murderer have been a doctor himself? Or a butcher or slaughterman?

The police received the first letter bearing the name Jack the Ripper a week later. It was considered a hoax, but the now famous 'Dear Boss' letter, posted on 25 September, appeared to be from the killer himself. The writer claimed he had collected the blood of his last victim in a ginger beer bottle and said he would have used it to write the letter if it had not become too thick. He also said he would cut the ears off his next victim and send them to the police.

At about 1am on Sunday 30 September Elizabeth Stride was murdered in a yard off Berner Street. It seems that a horse and cart pulling into the yard disturbed the killer, as after slashing the victim's throat he only had time to partially sever her ear before running away along Commercial Road. Half an hour later he struck again, and this time he had enough time to finish the job. Between police patrols through Mitre Square at 1.30am and 1.45am, Catherine Eddowes was murdered. Minutes before the body was found a policeman had seen a man coming out of an alley leading off Mitre Square, but had not stopped him. It was a frenzied attack, as if the killer was compensating for the earlier interruption. She had been disembowelled and her uterus and one of her

## HER THROAT HAD BEEN CUT DOWN TO THE BONE AND HER STOMACH SLASHED

kidneys were missing. A piece of her apron was found not far away. The killer had washed the blood off his hands and used it to clean them. On the wall above the apron graffiti had been scrawled. It said 'The Juwes are the men That Will not be Blamed for nothing'. The police assumed the killer was trying to blame Jewish people for the murders and they washed the graffiti off. A tide of anti-Semitism was already rising in the East End over the murders. After the first two killings local gossip had attributed them to a Jew, given the name Leather Apron, and there had already been demonstrations against the large Jewish community in the area. By taking the measures they did, the police, fearing reprisals against Jewish people, hoped to avoid inflaming the local population even more than they already were. In doing so they may have lost a vital piece of evidence.

The 'Saucy Jack' postcard arrived a few days later, calling the two murders the 'double event'. It was in the same handwriting as the 'Dear Boss' letter and gave details of the murders of Elizabeth Stride and Catherine Eddowes. Opinions were divided then, as they are today, about whether these letters were an elaborate hoax or if they where really written by the Ripper. Another letter was sent to George Lusk, Chairman of the Whitechapel Vigilance Committee, an organization set up after the police had failed to find the murderer. The 'From Hell' letter, as it is known, contained half a human kidney, the writer claiming to have eaten the other half. It contained numerous spelling mistakes and grammatical errors, seen by some as an attempt by an educated man to present himself as being all but illiterate.

The last of the five murders occurred on 9 November. Mary Jane Kelly had been seen late that night heading for her lodgings with a man. The next morning her landlord found her dismembered body in her room. The killer had taken his time. She was mutilated even more hideously than the previous victims had been. Her head was almost severed from her body and her face slashed until she was no longer recognizable. Her breasts and some of her flesh had been cut off and her internal organs pulled out and left in a pile next to her. The Ripper had cut out her heart and taken it away with him.

BELOW: The corpse of Elizabeth Stride.

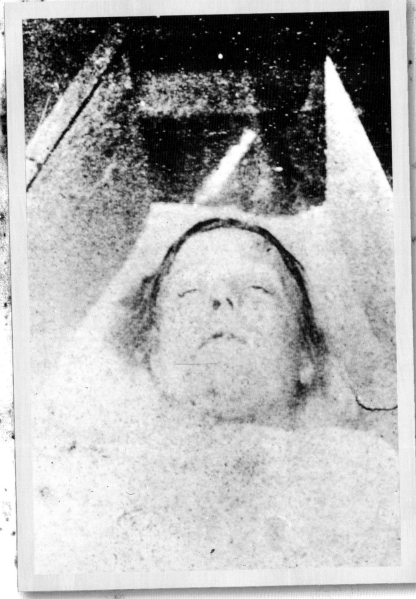

looked like, developed from contemporary descriptions given by witnesses, and there have been numerous reconstructions of his every known movement. Films continue to be made, most recently From Hell, starring Johnny Depp as Inspector Frederick Abberline, a prominent detective involved in the investigation, and based on a graphic novel.

In Whitechapel today it is possible to take Ripper tours of the sites of the murders and other places connected with the case. The tours usually end in The Ten Bells in Commercial Street, a pub known to have been frequented by several of the Ripper's victims and, if rumours are to be believed, by Jack the Ripper himself. For those who cannot get to Whitechapel, there are an enormous number of websites dedicated to Ripper studies, and there are also several societies of like-minded enthusiasts, which produce magazines containing articles by a growing band of amateur detectives.

Identifying new suspects as Jack the Ripper has become something of an industry in itself. The more high profile the person named as the latest suspect, the greater the publicity generated. In Victorian England, who could be more high profile than a member of the royal family? Prince Albert Victor, the Duke of Clarence, was Queen Victoria's grandson

Nothing further was ever heard from Jack the Ripper. At the time of the murders there was a huge amount of public interest. Newspapers were much more numerous and widely read than they had ever been before, and they fanned the flames of hysteria surrounding the case. It might have been expected that interest would diminish over time, as the period receded into history, but this is certainly not what has happened. The mystery of Jack the Ripper's identity continues to fascinate and intrigue successive generations of Ripperologists, as people who have become obsessed with the details of the murders are called. Countless books have been published on the subject, more than for any other true crime subject – with the possible exception of the assassination of John F Kennedy. TV documentaries have shown computer-generated photofits of what Jack the Ripper might have

and, in the 1970s, was proposed as being Jack the Ripper in a number of books. Unfortunately for the authors, the duke had a cast-iron alibi. He wasn't even in London when the majority of the murders were committed. Not to be put off, a conspiracy theory was then developed which suggested that Sir William Gull, Queen Victoria's doctor, was the Ripper. He committed the murders, according to the theory, to cover up an affair between Prince Albert and an East End prostitute that resulted in her becoming pregnant and giving birth to a potential heir to the throne. As a conspiracy theory it was a good one. As well as the royal family, almost every prominent politician, from the prime minister down, was involved, together with a host of other famous Victorians. Walter Sickert, who would later be accused of being the Ripper himself by the crime writer PD James, had a part to play, as did the Freemasons and any number of senior police officers. Elaborate as it was, this theory was based more on fantasy than fact and its claims were easily demolished when subjected to serious scrutiny.

One of the more convincing suspects identified in recent years is Joseph Barnett. He was Mary Ann Kelly's common-law husband and fitted the descriptions given by some witnesses. He was 1 m 70 cm (5 ft 7 in) tall, stockily built, dark haired with a moustache and a fair complexion. He had lived in the Whitechapel area all his life and must have known all the alleyways and back streets well, as the Ripper appeared to do, and he knew at least one of the other victims. A motive for the killings suggests Barnett could have been attempting to scare Kelly into giving up prostitution by killing other prostitutes and, when that didn't work, he killed Kelly as well. The Ripper had shown that he knew how to use a knife and, as Barnett worked as a porter in Billingsgate Fish Market, he would have developed the required skills through filleting and gutting fish. In his defence, he was questioned by the police after the Kelly murder and doesn't appear to have been regarded as a suspect by them. Also, serial killers very rarely stop killing until they are either caught or die, and Barnett continued to live in the Whitechapel area long after the killings stopped.

The case against Barnett is unproven, as it is for all the other suspects. Despite an enormous number of people attempting to solve the mystery, 120 years after the crimes were committed, a solution is as far away as ever. Short of a miraculous discovery of new evidence, which can be proved to be authentic – unlike the forged Ripper Diaries found a few years ago – it is hard to see how any further progress can be made. The Ripper's identity, like the man himself, continues to lurk in the shadows.

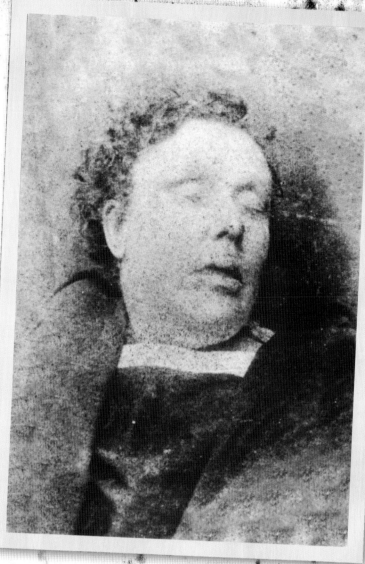

ABOVE: The corpse of Annie Chapman.
OPPOSITE PAGE: The corpse of Mary Ann Nicholls.

# COULD THE MURDERER HAVE BEEN A DOCTOR HIMSELF? OR A BUTCHER OR SLAUGHTERMAN?

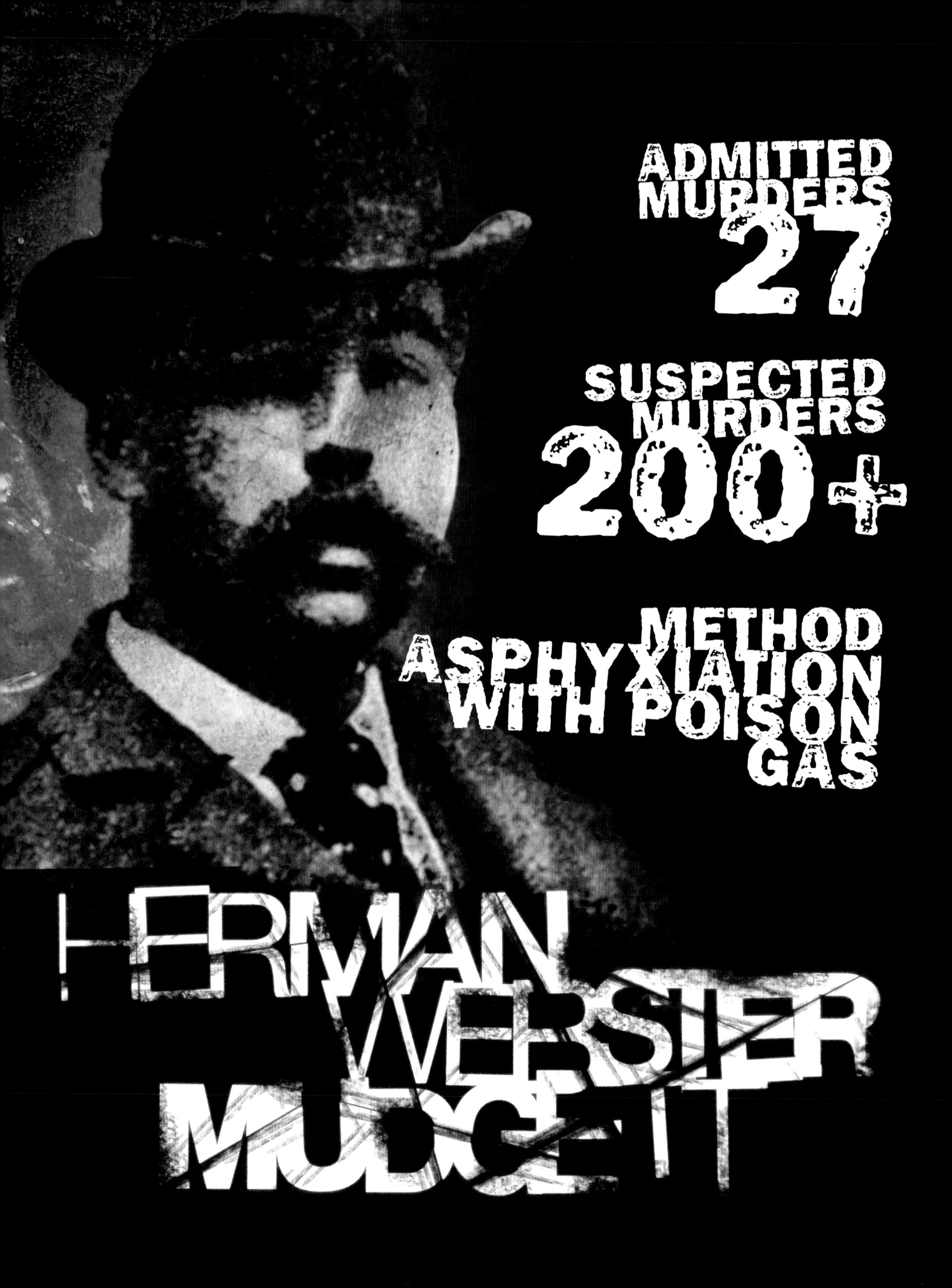

ADMITTED MURDERS
27

SUSPECTED MURDERS
200+

METHOD
ASPHYXIATION WITH POISON GAS

HERMAN WEBSTER MUDGETT

To enter the mind of **Herman Mudgett** would have been a fascinating, if not harrowing experience. How could a man appear to be an **upstanding member of the community**, a devoted husband and successful local businessman while concealing such **monstrous acts** of imprisonment, murder and mutilation?

The details of Herman Webster Mudgett's life are so bizarre and appalling as to be almost beyond belief. On the surface he was a successful doctor, pharmacist and businessman, but this facade concealed gruesome and macabre secrets which only came to light after he was investigated for insurance fraud. Eventually he confessed to the murder of 27 people, but, as he was a compulsive liar, it is impossible to know how much truth there was in his confession. Some estimates have put the true number at over 200.

Mudgett was born into an affluent family in Gilmanton, New Hampshire, in 1860. He studied medicine at the University of Michigan in Ann Arbor and, while still a student, began his criminal career with body-snatching. He would take out a life insurance policy under a bogus name, steal a corpse from a cemetery, disfigure it with acid so it could not be recognized and pass it off as the person insured. After almost being caught, he left Ann Arbor and assumed the name of Dr HH Holmes. He was involved in a variety of scams: more insurance fraud, forgery, embezzlement and, more than likely, murder, before he resurfaced as a pharmacist in Chicago. The owner of the pharmacy, an elderly widow, disappeared not long after he arrived, and he was left to run the business himself.

A string of successful ventures: selling a cure for alcoholism, inventing a machine to make natural gas, together with more fraud, made him a wealthy man. At about this time he married Myrta Belknap, no doubt neglecting to mention he had married a woman when he was eighteen and never divorced her. He built a large hotel with more than 100 rooms and opened it in time for the Chicago World's Fair in 1893. It had been built by a succession of different builders, so nobody except Holmes, as he was now called, knew about all the special features he had included in the building. There were secret passages, rooms with no windows and chutes leading down to the basement. Doors opened

# YOUNG, SINGLE FEMALE GUESTS WOULD STAY A FEW NIGHTS AND NEVER BE SEEN AGAIN

onto brick walls, staircases led to nowhere. Business was brisk with visitors coming to Chicago for the fair or to look for work and staying in this strange hotel, which became known as The Castle.

How many of the residents checked in but never checked out has never been accurately established. Young, single female guests would stay a few nights and never be seen again. Waitresses and chambermaids in the hotel would leave their jobs suddenly without saying goodbye. Meanwhile, Holmes was running a side business selling skeletons to doctors and university laboratories. He even had an assistant to help him strip the flesh off the bodies and prepare the skeletons for sale. The bodies were, he claimed, those of patients of his who had died.

No one appeared to have been suspicious of his activities. He was charming and gracious, particularly with women. He could talk his way out of settling the bills for the chemicals he used in his business and explain away the chemical smells coming out of the basement when guests in the hotel complained.

Eventually Holmes's many creditors demanded repayment of a large sum of money that he owed them. He duped a woman from Texas into transferring the title of the land she owned in Fort Worth to him and then killed both her and her sister, entered into another bigamous marriage and set fire to the hotel for the insurance, before skipping town with his new wife and Benjamin Pitezel, a man who worked for him in the hotel. Detectives from the Pinkerton Agency investigating various insurance claims trailed him to Fort Worth, St. Louis and on to Philadelphia, where they

finally caught up with him. He had been involved in yet another insurance scam with Benjamin Pitezel, who then disappeared. Holmes produced a body and tried to claim the insurance. It was one step too far. He was challenged and came up with a story saying the body wasn't Pitezel, suggesting he was committing insurance fraud not murder. One of Pitezel's daughters identified the body and Holmes was arrested for his murder. The Pinkerton agents continued to follow the trail Holmes had left, finding the bodies of Pitezel's wife and other members of his family in a house in Toronto, and the Chicago police began to investigate the hotel.

Inside they found airtight rooms with gas pipes running into them, and doors that could only be opened from the outside. They concluded that Holmes had killed people by asphyxiating them with gas. He then transferred the bodies down to the basement, where he had installed a dissecting table and acid baths. After selling the skeletons of his victims, he disposed of the remains of the bodies by cremating them and throwing them into lime pits. The police found various body parts in the basement, along with women's shoes and clothes.

Holmes was put on trial for Pitezel's murder, even though details of at least some of his other crimes were beginning to emerge. He was found guilty and sentenced to death. While awaiting execution he wrote a long and rambling confession to 27 murders and said he thought he was possessed by the devil. The *New York Times* reported his execution, saying he had been calm and collected immediately beforehand, asking the hangman to take his time and to do the job properly. The hangman doesn't appear to have listened and Holmes died slowly. After the trap in the gallows opened and he dropped to the end of the rope, it was 15 minutes before he was pronounced dead.

MURDER VICTIMS
11

METHOD
STRANGLE

EXECUTION
GUILLOTINE

HENRI
LANDRU

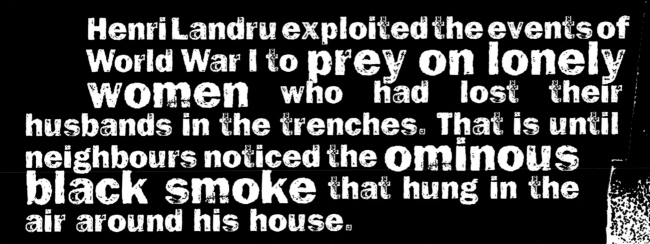

# Henri Landru exploited the events of World War I to prey on lonely women who had lost their husbands in the trenches. That is until neighbours noticed the ominous black smoke that hung in the air around his house.

For a man who could exert great influence over women, Henri Landru cut an odd figure. He was short, balding and sported a big bushy beard — hardly the typical appearance of a successful ladies' man. But he was charming and persuasive, and he would become a ladykiller in more than one sense of the phrase.

Landru came from a working-class district of northern Paris. After leaving school he served for four years in the army, rising to the rank of sergeant. He seduced his cousin and she became pregnant, but, on leaving the army, he abandoned her and married another woman, with whom he had four children. After being swindled by a man he worked for, he appears to have decided that crime was an easier way of making a living than doing an honest job. He set himself up as a second-hand furniture dealer and, when he met a widow who was selling her furniture, he attempted to persuade her to let him invest the money for her. The money would never be seen again and, if he had made the woman any promises, he would break them, sometimes leaving the woman penniless. The problem with this scam was that the women he stole money from knew who he was and some of them reported him to the police. He was arrested several times and was sent to prison to serve sentences for embezzlement and fraud.

By 1905 the plan had evolved. He placed lonely hearts adverts in newspapers under false names, saying he was a widower looking for companionship with a view to getting married. He received plenty of replies from lonely widows and used his considerable charm to persuade them to sign their money and possessions over to him. As the sums of money got bigger, so did the prison terms when he got caught. Although he used a false name, the women he swindled could still recognize him. In 1908 he received a three-year jail sentence and, while he was inside, both his parents died, his father committing suicide in despair at the dishonour his son had brought on the family. By the time Landru

got out, his wife had left him and taken the children with her. These personal setbacks appear to have relieved him of any sense of moral restraint, and, if he had a conscience, he no longer let it hinder him.

What Landru needed was to prevent the victims of his scams from going to the police. The obvious answer, at least to him, was to silence them permanently. With World War I claiming the lives of so many French men, there were more widows than ever for him to prey on. He could afford to be choosy, selecting the wealthier women who replied to his lonely hearts adverts. In December 1914 he met Jeanne Cuchet. She moved into the house he had bought in Dreux, a town to the west of Paris, with her sixteen-year-old son.

After January 1915, neither of them were seen again. With the country at war, there were few resources available to investigate their disappearance. By May he had met Thérèse Laborde-Line, and she also moved in with him, believing she was going to marry a man called Monsieur Cuchet.

In 1916 he moved to a villa near Gambais, nearer Paris, and bought a large new stove for the kitchen. The disappearances continued, but would not come to light until 1919, when the family of one of his victims, Célestine Buisson, tried to find her. They contacted the Mayor of Gambais, who could not help, but he put them in touch with the family of another missing woman. Together they contacted the police and the villa was searched. There was no trace of either woman. Then, by

Excavations in the cellar of a house in Vernouillet, rented by Landru.

an amazing stroke of good fortune, Célestine Buisson's sister saw Landru coming out of a shop in Paris. She had seen him before with Célestine and tried to follow him, but lost him on a crowded street. She had the presence of mind to go back to the shop to ask if they knew who he was. The name they had for him was different from the one she had, but they also had his address. She informed the police and he was immediately arrested. The house in Gambais was searched again, but the only item of interest found was a notebook where Landru had listed 11 names, including Célestine's. He had kept a record of his victims, together with the different aliases he had used. There were also details of their finances and his expenses. In one entry he made a note of train tickets he had bought from Paris to Gambais for himself and Madame Heon, another of the missing women. He had bought a return for himself and a single for her. No point in wasting money on a ticket he knew would not be used.

Although no bodies were found Landru was charged with 11 murders, based on the entries in the notebook. Believing he could not be found guilty by the evidence of the notebook alone, without any bodies, he decided to stay silent. The investigation continued for two years without making any significant progress, until local people mentioned they had occasionally noticed a noxious black smoke coming from one of the chimneys of the house. The police examined the stove in the kitchen, where they found burnt human bone fragments and the remains of the metal fastenings of women's clothing. They surmised that he had strangled the women before disposing of the bodies in the stove.

At his trial Landru continued to deny everything, and he refused to answer any of the questions put to him by the prosecution. He still believed he could not be found guilty if no bodies were found, and his lawyer argued that he had been involved in the white slave trade not in murder. The jury were having none of it and found him guilty. He was sentenced to death and sent to the guillotine on 25 February 1922. Almost 50 years later a confession apparently written by him was found. As he waited for his execution, he had drawn a picture and then given it to his lawyer. On the back of it he had written 'I did it. I burnt their bodies in my kitchen stove'.

Henri Landru during his trial in in 1921.

MURDER VICTIMS
27+

METHOD
BITING
VICTIMS'
THROAT

A.K.A.
THE
BUTCHER
OF
HANOVER

FRITZ
HAARMANN

# The stomach-turning crimes

Fritz Haarmann committed will no doubt remain in the minds of Hanoverians for generations to come. The Butcher of Hanover sold meat on Germany's black market, but what his customers thought was knock-off pork or beef was in fact something quite different, and not at all nice.

At the end of World War I, Germany was in economic meltdown. The allies had blockaded German ports throughout the war and food was scarce. Meat, in particular, was hard to get and, when it was available, it was rationed and expensive. In 1918 in Hanover, Fritz Haarmann began to sell beef and pork on the black market and, along with his homosexual lover Hans Grans, also made money selling second-hand clothes. It would be six years before the connection between these two money-making schemes was exposed. Haarmann had been picking up homeless boys and young male prostitutes, killing them, butchering their bodies and selling their flesh as pork or beef. Germany had just been through the wholesale slaughter of World War I, but, even so, the horrific nature of Haarmann's crimes shocked and appalled the country. Even worse, the citizens of Hanover knew that a good number of them had unknowingly eaten human flesh, and it looked as if the Hanover police had been turning a blind eye to Haarmann's gruesome activities for years.

Haarmann had an unhappy and troubled childhood. His father was emotionally distant and domineering and his mother was overprotective and manipulative. In more recent times in America, the FBI have developed psychological profiles of serial killers and have, in almost every case, found a similar pattern of childhood trauma as that experienced by Haarmann. The first signs of the trouble to come appeared when he was sixteen. He was accused of sexually molesting younger children and spent six months in a mental institution. After a failed engagement and a short spell in the army, from which he was honourably discharged on health grounds, he fell into the life of a petty criminal in Hanover. He became well known to the police after being arrested a number of times on a variety of minor charges.

In 1914 he was sent to prison for the burglary of a warehouse and spent the majority of the war years behind bars. On his release he returned to a life of crime, but this time he also became a police informer. He was involved in the black market and, while he continued to provide useful information, he was allowed to get away with it. The first signs of what he was really doing emerged in 1918. Had the police chosen to investigate him thoroughly then, they could have prevented the horrors that were to come. But he was a protected man and the police didn't want to lose the information he was giving them. Friedel Rothe, a seventeen-year-old boy, had gone missing and had been tracked to Haarmann's apartment by his father. The police were called and they found Haarmann in bed with a thirteen-year-old boy. He was arrested for indecency with a minor, for which he would spend nine months in prison, but the police found no sign of Rothe. At his trial six years later, Haarmann would claim that Rothe's head was in the apartment at the

time of his arrest. He said it was in a paper bag behind the stove.

While in prison, Haarmann met Hans Grans, a homosexual pimp. On their release, Grans became Haarmann's accomplice, as well as his lover. They picked up homeless boys who were hanging around the railway station and took them back to their apartment. Haarmann had sex with them and, while he was in some sort of sexual frenzy, he bit the boys in the throat, ripping out their carotid arteries. The boys bled to death and Haarmann butchered their bodies, dumping the body parts he could not sell in the nearby River Leine. Grans took their clothes and sold them.

Local residents alerted the police to some strange goings on at the apartment. Boys were often seen going into the apartment, but were rarely seen coming out. Haarmann was seen disposing of buckets of blood, and Grans was selling blood-stained clothing. The police did nothing. It was as if they had gone beyond protecting him and were now colluding in his crimes.

In May 1924 children playing by the river found human bones. Initially the police dismissed the finds as some sort of sick joke, perhaps perpetrated by medical students. More bones were found, including a human skull, and the police still did nothing. Then a bag of bones was found in the river and rumours of there being hundreds of boys missing in Hanover spread like wildfire. The police could not stall any longer and, finally, an investigation began. The river was dredged

## HAARMANN HAD SEX WITH THEM AND, WHILE HE WAS IN SOME SORT OF SEXUAL FRENZY, HE BIT THE BOYS IN THE THROAT, RIPPING OUT THEIR CAROTID ARTERIES

Fritz Haarmann walks from jail to the court house for sentencing.

and the remains of more than 20 boys were found. Suspicion immediately fell on Haarmann and the authorities called in detectives from Berlin, not trusting the local police to run the investigation properly. The detectives followed Haarmann and watched him attempting to pick up a boy at the railway station. He was arrested and his apartment searched. Inside the apartment they found bloodstains on the floor and walls. Haarmann tried to explain it away as the result of his activities as a black-market butcher. He could not explain the clothes and personal effects of some of the missing boys they also found.

The identities of 27 boys were established from what the detectives found in the apartment, and Haarmann was charged with their murders. These only accounted for the boys known to have been killed since the start of 1923, and there were undoubtedly many more murders before then. Haarmann admitted the murders he was charged with, but said he could not remember how many boys he had killed in total. He also implicated Grans, who was charged with complicity to murder. It didn't take the jury long to find both of them guilty. Haarmann was sentenced to death and was beheaded in Hanover Prison on 15 April 1925. Grans served 12 years of a life sentence. After his release he is thought to have continued to live in Hanover, until his death in the 1980s.

MURDER VICTIMS
10+

METHOD
STAB
BLUDGEON
HAMMER

EXECUTION
GUILLOTINE

PETER KURTEN

Like many of his serial killing kind, neighbours described Peter Kürten as a meek, god-fearing, church going family man. Little did they know that this mild-mannered act masked the actions of a **sexually deviant psychopath** who would stop at nothing in his mission to terrorize the women of Düsseldorf.

The case of Peter Kürten represents something of a watershed in the investigation of serial killers. Before he was executed, Kürten was interviewed by Professor Karl Berg, a psychiatrist, who built up what would now be called a psychological profile. He described Kürten as a narcissistic psychopath and a sexual pervert. It was 15 years before Berg's work became widely known outside Germany, but it was the first time the technique of profiling had been applied to such crimes and, in later years, it would become a central tenet in the investigation and capture of many other serial killers.

Kürten talked openly and extensively about his life and crimes with Professor Berg, and the details revealed would be ones which would crop up again and again in the lives of other serial killers. Kürten's father was an alcoholic who regularly beat him and sexually abused his mother and sister in front of him. In his early teens he helped a dog catcher to kill stray dogs and began to derive sexual pleasure from torturing them to death. He became an arsonist, setting fire to people's houses to see the reaction the fire would get, and there were suggestions he had tried to kill young children by drowning them when he was swimming in a river. After the family moved from Cologne to Düsseldorf, he got a string of jobs but couldn't hold on to any of them and so he began a career as a petty criminal. The

police arrested him for theft and minor sexual offences, and he served a number of terms in prison. Gradually the scale of his offending increased. In May 1913 he committed the first of his known murders, killing a thirteen-year-old girl he chanced upon after he had broken into a house. He strangled her and then cut her throat with a pocket knife. The girl's uncle was charged with the murder and, although he was acquitted, rumours persisted about him. He died a broken man a few years later. No doubt Kürten looked on from a distance, enjoying the effect his crime had on others, as he had done as an arsonist. A few months later he killed another young girl. This time he strangled her while they were having sex.

World War I stopped this first killing spree. He was drafted into the army and deserted almost immediately. He was caught and sentenced to eight years in prison. By the time he got out, in 1921, he appeared to be a changed man. He moved away from Düsseldorf, got married and found a steady job. When asked about him after his arrest, neighbours described him as a mild-mannered church-goer. It was not until he moved back to Düsseldorf that his second killing spree began. It was as if being back in the surroundings where he had killed before had set him off once again.

The pattern developed in the same way. Petty crime, arson, followed by opportunist attacks on women. It was several years before he began to kill again. In February 1929 he attacked a woman in the street, stabbing her 24 times without actually killing her. A week later he raped and murdered an eight-year-old girl. He stabbed her repeatedly with a pair of scissors and hid her body on a building site, returning later and attempting to dispose of the remains by burning them. It was the beginning of a reign of terror in Düsseldorf that would last until he was finally caught a year later.

Attacks continued regularly, not all of them fatal. The police didn't appear to have any idea who the madman was, and the newspapers dubbed him the Vampire of Düsseldorf and wrote lurid stories about him drinking the blood of his victims. Two girls, one 13, the other 5, were killed at the same time. One was strangled and the other had her throat cut. The city was in a state of panic. Several of the women who survived attacks

## HE TOLD PROFESSOR BERG ABOUT THE PLEASURE HE GOT FROM HURTING PEOPLE AND HOW THE SIGHT OF BLOOD MADE HIM SEXUALLY EXCITED

gave accurate descriptions of Kürten to the police, but they made no progress in finding the murderer.

Towards the end of September Kürten changed his method. Perhaps too many people were surviving after he stabbed them with a knife or scissors. Whatever the reason, he began to bludgeon his victims to death with a hammer. He began to send details of where the bodies were to the police, in imitation of Jack the Ripper, who, he would later say, he held in great admiration. In May 1930 he attacked Maria Budlies. He first talked her into coming to his apartment, where he attempted to rape her. He then took her into some nearby woods and attacked her again, but didn't kill her. Initially she didn't report the attack to the police, but wrote to a friend about it. The letter was wrongly addressed and was opened in the post office to try to discover the address of the sender. The details of the attack it contained were passed on to the police and they persuaded her to show them where her attacker lived. Kürten evaded arrest at first, but, after admitting his crimes to his wife, she turned him in and he was arrested.

Kürten was charged with nine murders and seven attempted murders. He confessed and gave details to the police of many more crimes. At his trial he entered a plea of insanity, but this was rejected and he was found guilty on all charges. He told Professor Berg about the pleasure he got from hurting people, and how the sight of blood made him sexually excited. On 2 July 1931 he was sent to the guillotine, where, just before being beheaded, he asked his executioner if he would live long enough after his head was cut off to be able to hear the blood gushing out of his body.

OPPOSITE PAGE: A dressmaker's dummy dressed in the clothes of one of Kürten's victims.
BELOW: A sketch by Kürten, indicating where the body of Gertrude Albernamm would be found.

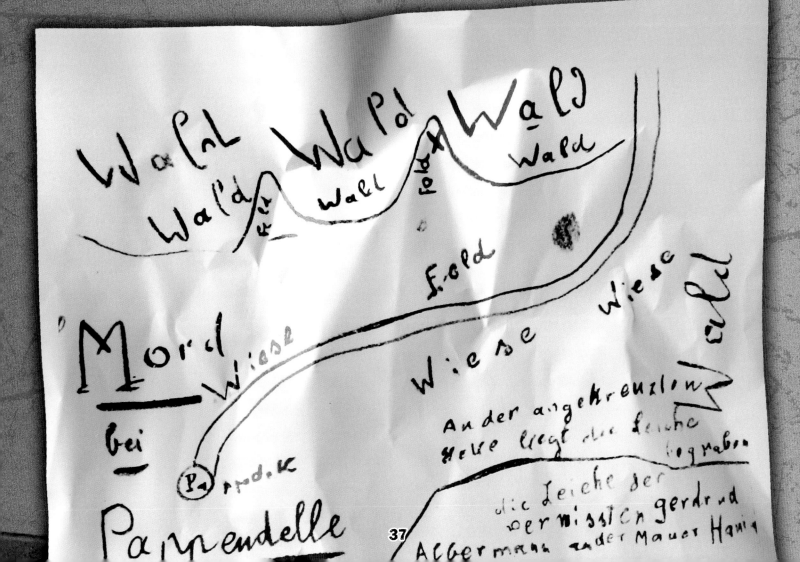

MURDER VICTIMS **8**

METHOD **STRANGLE**

EXECUTION **HANGED**

JOHN REGINALD CHRISTIE

**Reginald Christie was an acutely intelligent, well-spoken man who used his charm and intellect to dupe backward Timothy Evans into taking the rap for the murder of his precious wife and child. As it turned out, the murders of Beryl Evans and her daughter Geraldine were just the tip of the iceberg. Christie's kitchen cupboards would reveal many more.**

In January 1950 Timothy Evans was put on trial at the Old Bailey in London for the murder of his wife Beryl Evans, and their fourteen-month-old daughter Geraldine. He had given himself up to the police and confessed to the murders, which had occurred in the top floor flat of 10 Rillington Place in Notting Hill. The two bodies were found in the communal outside wash house, rather than in a drain, where Evans said he had hidden them, but that was considered to be a minor detail. Timothy Evans was undoubtedly one of life's unfortunates. Undersized with a mental age of just 10 or 11, he also liked a drink and was known to tell elaborate stories in order to boost his faltering self-confidence. He and his young family were very poor but they had been happy during their time together. The arrival of their baby, and news of a second child on the way, had put huge financial strain on Evans, but Geraldine was generally loved and cared for by both her parents. The lack of money had caused quarrels between husband and wife, and Beryl was desperate to abort her second child, a practice that was still illegal at the time, but did this strain drive Timothy Evans to murder?

The chief prosecution witness was John Reginald Halliday Christie, a man who had served in the army in World War I and had joined the War Reserve Police in 1939. He lived in the ground floor flat of the house with his wife Ethel and testified to having heard frequent rows between Evans and his wife. In court he was quietly spoken and answered questions in a considered way. He looked like a respectable member of the community. Evans, in contrast, came across as nervous and inarticulate. He kept muttering 'Christie done it', but nobody believed him, not even his defence counsel. The jury returned a guilty verdict and Evans was hanged on 5 March.

# HE KEPT MUTTERING 'CHRISTIE DONE IT'

ABOVE: Timothy Evans.
OPPOSITE PAGE: Christie arriving at court in London to face murder charges, 8 April 1953.

The police were convinced of Evans's guilt from the outset and, in all likelihood, coerced a confession out of him. Had they investigated the case more thoroughly they might have avoided a grave miscarriage of justice. In 1966, 13 years after the full extent of the crimes committed at 10 Rillington Place had come to light, Evans would be granted a posthumous free pardon.

It is now widely believed that Ethel and Reginald Christie heard about Beryl's desperate wish for an abortion and Reginald approached Evans promising he could help. He showed Evans a book supposedly describing an operation he could perform on Beryl. It is unlikely that the book contained any such information, as the only medical books found in the house were first-aid books, but Evans was illiterate – a fact that seemed to have escaped the court's notice during his trial. Newspaper cuttings detailing the Stanley Setty torso murder were submitted as evidence for the prosecution, having been found in Evans's flat. Evidence that could easily have been planted by Christie.

Christie explained that there were risks attached to the operation, and one in ten patients died during surgery. Evans apparently said he was not interested, but Beryl was adamant to go ahead with the abortion and so she did, with disastrous consequences. On Tuesday 8 November Evans went to work as usual. When he returned Christie greeted him with bad news. Beryl had died during the 'operation'. Her body had been laid out on the bed. There was blood on her mouth and nose, which Christie apparently attributed to the 'bottom part'. Christie told Evans to stay in the kitchen while he disposed of the body.

Christie also told Evans, who was now facing life as a single parent, that he knew a couple in East Acton who could take Geraldine in. He supposedly arranged for the couple to come and collect Geraldine the very next day while Evans was out at work. Evans made arrangements to leave London and return to his native Wales. The body of young Geraldine Evans was later found by police in the washroom near to Beryl's body.

It seems that the only crime Timothy Evans was guilty of was one of extreme naivety. In fact one could argue that

Evans was also Christie's victim, since, if there is any truth in the accepted version of events, Evans was not only robbed of his wife and both his children, but his reputation as a law-abiding citizen and ultimately, via the court, of his own life. It is certainly true that Christie was highly intelligent and would have been able to manipulate Evans with great ease.

Three years after Evans's trial and subsequent death, Reginald Christie moved out of his flat in Rillington Place. The landlord allowed one of the other tenants, Beresford Brown, who had recently arrived in Britain from Jamaica, to use the kitchen in the unoccupied flat. There was a terrible smell in the flat and Brown set about cleaning up the kitchen. He found that someone, presumably Christie, had wallpapered over a cupboard, so he stripped the paper off and opened it, to be confronted by the body of a woman. Behind her were two more bodies wrapped in blankets, one stacked on top of the other.

The police identified the bodies as Rita Nelson, Kathleen Maloney and Hectorina MacLennan. All three had been prostitutes and were killed within a few weeks of each other, all had been strangled with a length of rope. Ethel Christie's body was found next, under the floorboards in the bedroom. In the backyard they found a human leg bone propping up the garden fence and uncovered the remains of two more women, Ruth Fuerst and Muriel Eady. Both women had gone missing during World War II and were thought to have been killed in air raids. Christie had been a special constable during this time. As a figure of respect he would have had ample opportunity to spend time alone with women in the community, without ever arousing suspicion. If the authorities had checked his background when he originally joined the force, they would have uncovered multiple convictions for theft, larceny and assault. It appears that they too fell for his outwardly respectable appearance and manner, just as others had.

# IN THE BACKYARD THEY FOUND A HUMAN LEG BONE PROPPING UP THE GARDEN FENCE

A nationwide manhunt began for Christie. He had not gone very far. After moving out of the flat he stayed in a local shelter for the homeless, using his own name, and when he had run out of money he slept in parks and on the Thames Embankment. A policeman recognized him from a photograph and arrested him. Although he had made attempts to disguise himself, he behaved almost as if he had wanted to be caught and was relieved when he was.

Christie's early life had been troubled. As a child he had lived in fear of his violent father and grandfather and was dominated by his mother and bossy older sisters. At the age of eight his grandfather died and attending his wake appears to have had a major psychological affect on Christie. His grandfather could not hurt him in death, so instead of being afraid, he now felt powerful and in control. Christie later described feelings of fascination and pleasure upon encountering his grandfather's corpse. He took to playing in local graveyards – perhaps because he had begun to associate the presence of death with feelings of safety and security.

To add to his confusion and distress, Christie's first sexual encounter was nothing short of a disaster. The girl involved took pleasure in telling anyone who would listen how inadequate his efforts had been. This, teamed with frustrating relationships with his female family members, seems to have initiated in Christie a barely concealed hatred of the female gender. Later in life he appears to have begun to associate death with sex. He could only have sex successfully when he felt totally in control of the situation. When he didn't, he became impotent. Christie didn't admit to having sex with the dead bodies of the women he killed, but psychologists suggest this could well have been his primary motivation for killing them. Most of Christie's prostitute victims had been rendered unconscious

ABOVE: The run-down garden of number 10 Rillington Place, London

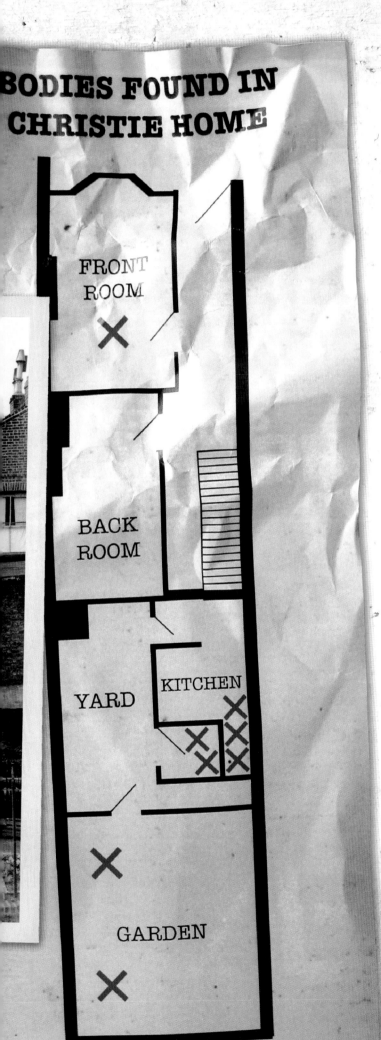

## BODIES FOUND IN CHRISTIE HOME

FRONT ROOM

✗

BACK ROOM

YARD

KITCHEN

✗
✗ ✗
✗ ✗
✗ ✗

GARDEN

✗

✗

with gas from the domestic supply before they were strangled, but it could not be confirmed for certain if he'd had sex with them when they were alive or dead. Bearing in mind Christie's known fascination with death, and the feelings of power and pleasure it aroused in him, the latter is highly likely. It is worth noting that Christie was known to have sexually neglected his wife, while he regularly visited prostitutes. He always maintained that the women he killed had forced themselves on him, rather than the other way around. How that was possible since a number of them were gassed before being strangled is unclear. It appears that this was a part of Christie's own reality, something he had convinced himself of during, or soon after the kill. It is also worth noting that the murder of Christie's wife, Ethel, was not a sexually motivated one. The couple's relationship had completely broken down in the years before her death, they had frequent rows and both began to suffer from nervous tension. It seems that Ethel, having served whatever purpose Christie had in mind for her, was killed simply because she'd become a nuisance. The postmortem found no evidence of recent sexual intercourse.

As he was confronted with the evidence of his crimes, Christie began a series of confessions, changing them repeatedly as more damning evidence came to light. He confessed to killing Beryl Evans, but maintained he was innocent of killing her daughter. He tried to insinuate that his mental health had been affected by the injuries he had received during World War I. He was only charged with the murder of his wife Ethel, and, at his trial, entered a plea of insanity. The trial lasted four days and the jury, rejecting his plea because of the calculating way he went about the murder, found him guilty. An inquiry into his mental health agreed with the jury and Christie was sentenced to death. He was hanged two weeks after the sentence was passed, despite attempts to delay the execution so he could be questioned further about the other murders.

The authorities, it appeared, had no desire to revisit the Timothy Evans case. Both the police and the courts preferred to allow a miscarriage of justice to stand than admit to having made mistakes that led to the execution of the wrong man. The case was one of the driving forces behind the abolition of the death penalty in Britain. Had Evans received a jail sentence, it is almost certain he would have been released after Christie's conviction.

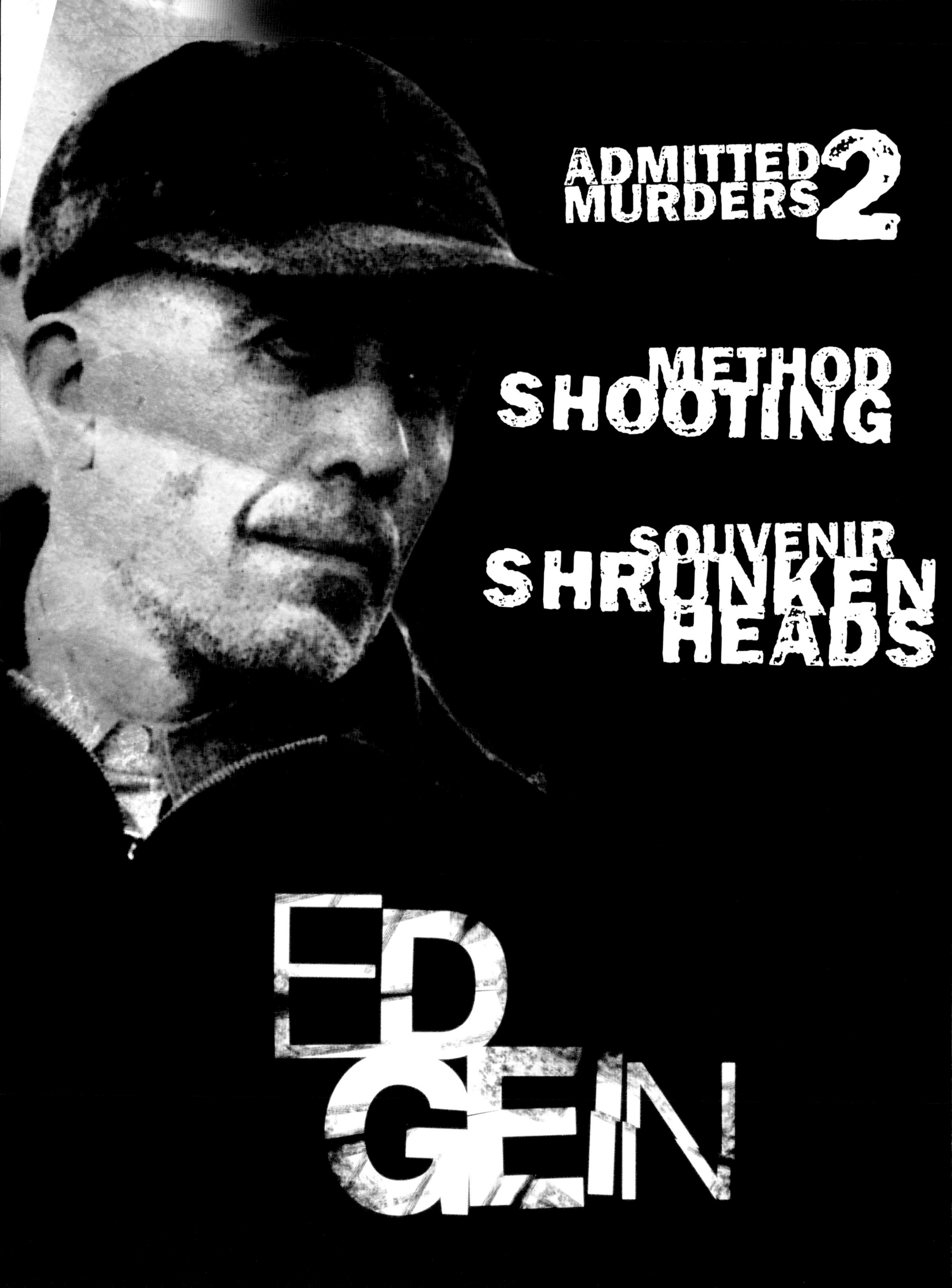

ADMITTED MURDERS **2**

METHOD
SHOOTING

SOUVENIR
SHRUNKEN
HEADS

ED
GEIN

# Ed Gein was the real-life Norman Bates. Obsessed with contacting his deceased mother, he was driven to kill, mutilate, dismember and bodysnatch his way through the small agricultural community of Plainfield, Wisconsin. Having ended his life confined to a hospital for the criminally insane, he will go down in history as one of the most twisted minds of the 20th century.

Plainfield, Wisconsin, is a small rural town with a population of about a thousand people – much the same now as it was in the 1950s. One day in the winter of 1952, Victor Travis and Ray Burgess stopped at the one bar in the town for a drink before they headed off to go deer hunting, a popular sport in the area. It was the last time either of them were seen. The state police had already noticed an increase in the number of missing persons from rural areas of Wisconsin, and these were two more to add to the list. Two years later, in December 1954, Mary Hogan, the owner of the bar, disappeared. Deputies from the sheriff's office found a rifle shell in the bar and a trail of blood leading out to the car park at the back. The trail led up to where a pickup truck had been parked, the tyre marks of which were left in the snow.

On 16 November 1957 Bernice Worden went missing from the hardware store she ran in town. As with Mary Hogan, there was a trail of blood leading out through the back door of the store. The last person seen in the store was Ed Gein, and a receipt for antifreeze in his name was found on the counter. He lived alone on a farm on the outskirts of town and was often seen around doing odd jobs. He was quiet and mostly kept himself to himself, he was thought of as being a little strange, but entirely harmless.

Deputies headed out to the farm to ask Gein if he had any information about the disappearance and stumbled across a scene of unimaginable horror. In a shed adjoining the house they found the headless body of a woman. She had been strung up by the heels to a beam, gutted and butchered in the same

way as a deer would have been. Horrendous as it was, this was only the beginning. The inside of the house was in a terrible state and the stench was almost unbearable. They found Bernice Worden's head in the kitchen, prepared as if it was going to be mounted on the wall as a trophy, and there was a heart in a pan on the cooker. Tanned human skin had been used to make seat covers and lampshades, and the top part of a skull was shaped into a soup bowl. In the bedroom there was a row of nine shrunken heads on the wall, including Mary Hogan's, and there were skulls on the bedposts. As if this was not horrific enough, they found an apron made from the gutted torso of a woman, with the breasts still attached, several pairs of leggings fashioned from skin and a mask made from a human face. The basement looked like a slaughterhouse. There were decaying body parts and entrails all over the place.

Forensic investigators found the remains of what they believed were at least 15 different women in the house. At first Gein denied everything, but,

when confronted with such overwhelming evidence, admitted killing Mary Hogan and Bernice Worden, but said he had stolen the other bodies from the local cemetery. When asked if he'd had sex with the bodies, he is said to have recoiled at the thought, saying they smelled far too bad for that. He was found to be mentally incompetent and was committed to a secure institution. Ten years later he was considered to have recovered sufficiently to stand trial, but the judge again ruled him to be insane. He spent the rest of his life in the Mendota Mental Health Institute where, according to the staff there, he was a model patient. He died there at the age of 77 from a heart attack.

Gein moved to the farm in Plainfield with his family in 1913. His mother, Augusta Gein, was a domineering woman with extremely strict religious views. She considered everyone else, particularly other women, to be evil and, as much as she could, prevented her two sons, Henry and Ed, from having anything to do with the outside world. She was married to George Gein, a chronic alcoholic who would regularly become

# THE WOMEN HE KILLED REMINDED HIM OF HIS MOTHER AND, BY KILLING THEM, HE FELT AS IF HE POSSESSED THEM

ABOVE: Augusta Gein's room at the farm in Plainfield, Winsconsin which Ed Gein left unused after her death in 1945.
LEFT: A deputy sheriff standing outside Ed Gein's house in Plainfield, Wisconsin.

violent. Augusta Gein despised him, but her religion prevented her from leaving him. It didn't prevent her praying for his death in front of her two sons. George Gein died of cirrhosis of the liver in 1940, and Henry Gein died fighting a brush fire a few years later. He was found dead with bruises on his face, but the exact circumstances of his death were not investigated, the coroner recording it as death by asphyxiation.

Augusta Gein suffered a stroke in 1945 and was looked after by her surviving son until she had a further stroke and died. After the funeral Ed Gein closed up the rooms in the house she had used, leaving everything as it had been when she was alive. His subsequent actions appear to have involved acting out ghoulish rituals to try and bring his mother back by pretending to be her. By digging up the corpses of middle-aged women in the graveyard and making

items of clothing from their bodies he was, in his twisted mind, trying to find a connection to her. The women he killed reminded him of his mother and, by killing them, he felt as if he possessed them. He had developed a very bizarre and gruesome mother fixation.

In 1959 Robert Bloch wrote the novel *Psycho*, which Alfred Hitchcock would film in the following year. Bloch claimed he only noticed the similarities between his Norman Bates character and Ed Gein after he had finished the book, but, as he lived in Wisconsin, this seems a little unlikely. Elements of Ed Gein have cropped up a number of other times in writing and the cinema. Buffalo Bill in *The Silence of the Lambs* and Leatherface in *The Texas Chainsaw Massacre* are two notable examples. Anyone needing a mother-obsessed madman for a character, it seems, need look no further than Ed Gein.

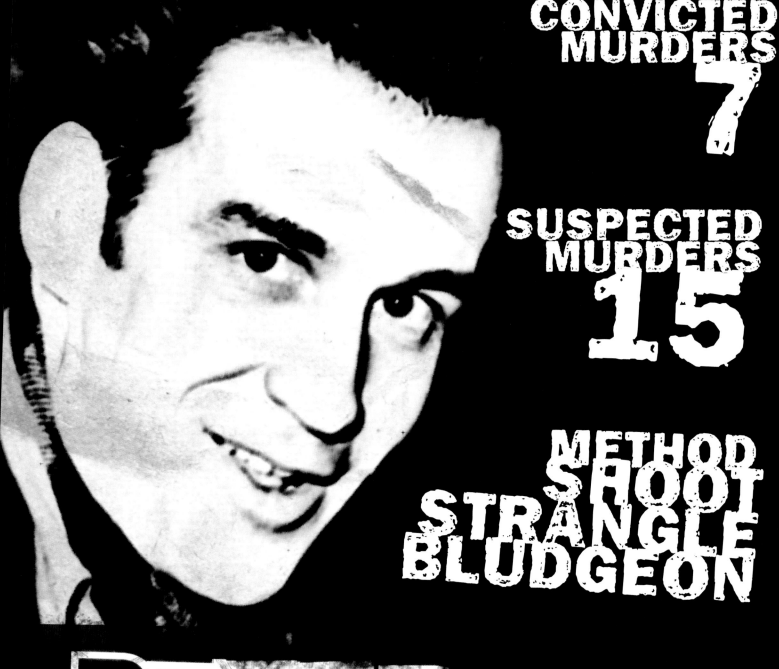

CONVICTED MURDERS **7**

SUSPECTED MURDERS **15**

METHOD
SHOOT
STRANGLE
BLUDGEON

PETER MANUEL

# Peter Manuel was an angry young man who remorselessly murdered anyone who got in his way – terrorizing the streets of Glasgow throughout the 1950s. He claimed insanity as a defence for the crimes he'd committed, but the judge did not accept Manuel's plea and he paid with his neck.

Glasgow was a rough town in the 1950s, but the spate of brutal killings committed by Peter Manuel between his first known murder in 1956 and his arrest in January 1958 shocked the city and the rest of the country. People who came into contact with him after his arrest all commented on his callous attitude and the complete indifference he showed to the charges brought against him. Unlike the majority of cases of serial killing, there was no discernible pattern to the murders Manuel committed. He didn't target a particular group of vulnerable people or use the same method for each murder. He killed people whenever they got in his way and used whatever means were at hand.

Manuel was born in New York into a family of Scottish expatriates. The family returned to the UK when he was five, settling in Coventry. He was a difficult child, who didn't make friends with other children easily, and he spent most of his time on his own. During his teenage years he developed into what was then called a juvenile delinquent. He was constantly in trouble for a string of minor offences, particularly theft and burglary, and was sent to young offenders' institutes and borstal a number of times. As he got older, the offences began to get more serious. Before he went to live with his parents in 1953, who had moved to Birkenshaw in the east end of Glasgow, he had served time in prison for sexual assault and rape.

The first murder which can definitely be attributed to Manuel came in 1956. He attacked a seventeen-year-old girl called Anna Knielands with an iron bar, bludgeoning her to death and leaving her body on one of the fairways of East Kilbride Golf Course. Manuel was well known to the police in Glasgow by this time and was brought in for questioning about the murder. Always a convincing liar, he talked his way out of any suspicion he may have been under and was released without charge. A few months later he was arrested for the burglary of a colliery near Glasgow and, while he was out on bail awaiting trial, he broke into a house in High Burnside and killed the three people he found inside. A postman found the bodies of two sisters, Marion Watt and Margaret Brown, and Watt's sixteen-year-old daughter Vivienne, on his rounds the following day. All three had been shot in the head at close range. Manuel was questioned again and released without charge. Suspicion then fell on Marion Watt's husband William, who was held in custody for two months before police established his innocence and released him.

At his trial for the colliery burglary Manuel was found guilty and received an 18-month prison sentence. It interrupted his killing spree, but it certainly didn't stop it. He was released in November 1957 and, on 29 December, he killed seventeen-year-old Isabella Cooke. She had left her flat that evening to go to meet

her boyfriend and didn't arrive. The next day she was reported missing. On New Year's Day 1958, Manuel shot Peter and Doris Smart and their ten-year-old son Michael in their home in Uddingston, a village a few miles outside Glasgow.

Manuel was caught 12 days later when a barman in a local pub grew suspicious of him and called the police. He had been buying drinks using money from a bundle of brand new notes. The police traced the serial numbers of the notes back to a payment that had been made to Peter Smart. After his arrest he took the police to the field where he had buried Isabella Cooke. As they were standing in the field, he was asked where exactly the body was buried. 'I'm standing on her now', he said.

FROM LEFT TO RIGHT: Mrs Martha Kneilands, mother of Anne Kneilands. Alice Kneilands, sister of Anne Kneilands. Inspector William Woods of Lanarkshire Police

# HE WAS ASKED WHERE EXACTLY THE BODY WAS BURIED "I'M STANDING ON HER NOW"

ABOVE: Peter Manuel is led away by police following his arrest for murder, 17 January 1958.

Although thought to have committed other murders, Manuel was charged with eight. At his trial in Glasgow High Court in May 1958, he conducted his own defence. He entered a plea of insanity, but, although he is said to have been surprisingly articulate, he failed to convince the judge and the plea was dismissed. He was found guilty on seven of the eight charges, the judge instructing the jury to acquit him of the murder of Anna Knielands even though he had confessed to the killing. The judge, Lord Cameron, would later write that he could detect no illness or abnormality in Manuel 'beyond callousness, selfishness and treachery in high degree'. He went on to say he thought Manuel's defence had been based on a calculating attempt to show he was not a criminal, but a man in need of medical care.

Lord Cameron passed sentence on Manuel, to be hanged by the neck until dead. Before going to the gallows, he confessed to the murders and to several others he had not been charged with, although this may have been an attempt to delay the execution. He was hanged in Barlinnie Prison on 11 July 1958, the penultimate execution in Scotland before the death penalty was abolished. He appeared as unconcerned for his own life as he had for the lives of his victims, asking the hangman to turn the radio up just before he was hanged. *The Scotsman* newspaper reported that 'a black cloud of terror has been lifted from the west of Scotland'.

The police and other people connected with the case believed Manuel had committed at least another eight murders besides those he was convicted for. It is impossible to know how many people he actually killed, but he remains one of the most cold-blooded killers in British history, killing for no other reason than he thought he could get away with it and, after he was caught, showing no signs of remorse for his crimes and the devastation he left behind.

MURDERS
3

METHOD
STRANGLE

EXECUTION
GAS
CHAMBER

HARVEY
GLATMAN

# Harvey Glatman was a souvenir collector who used photography to record his murders for posterity – and to prolong the thrill of the kill. The source of his pleasure would be his undoing, but unfortunately it all came too late for the models he hired to pose for 'magazine shoots', whose bodies he dumped unceremoniously in the desert.

Although not as infamous as many later serial killers, the case of Harvey Glatman changed the way serial crime was investigated in America. It would be another ten years before the term 'serial killer' would be coined, and ten more before it entered the public lexicon, but the crimes Glatman committed were recognized as following a pattern and were investigated as such. The propensity of serial killers to take something from the scene of the crime, to remind them of the thrill of it, was also first noted with the Glatman case. Glatman was described as a souvenir killer – he took photographs of his victims before and after he killed them so he could relive the sexual pleasure the murders aroused in him.

One trait he didn't share with almost every other serial killer was an abusive childhood. His mother could be described as being over-protective, but she comes across more as being deeply concerned and long-suffering over the trouble her son kept getting into. Glatman was born in 1927 in the Bronx. He was considered a good student at school, but found relationships

53

with other students, particularly girls, difficult. He began to retreat into a fantasy world and, by the time his parents moved to Denver when he was eleven, was already showing signs of an obsession with ropes and bondage. At this early age he discovered auto-erotic asphyxiation, throttling himself with a rope to heighten the pleasure of masturbation. A bad case of acne, large protruding ears and a generally scruffy appearance didn't help him with girls, who teased him as being a loser and a creep.

By the time Glatman was sixteen he was breaking into private residences. In one break-in he stole a handgun. From then on he stalked young women he was attracted to, following them to their homes, breaking in and forcing them at gunpoint to strip in front of him. One of his victims went to the police and picked him out of the mugshots they showed her. He was arrested and given a 12-month prison sentence. After he got out, his parents found him a flat in Yonkers, New York, to get him away from Denver and the stigma of being a sex offender. He got a job in a TV repair shop, but it wasn't long before he was attacking women again. After a series of muggings, he was caught. There was no sexual element to the attacks, but, as he was a repeat offender, he was sentenced to five to ten years in prison. At first he was sent to a reformatory and then transferred to Sing Sing, the notorious maximum-security prison.

A psychiatrist described him as having a psychopathic personality, with possible schizophrenic tendencies, but he proved himself to be a model prisoner. After three years he was released on parole under his parents' supervision. For the next three years he appears to have lived a relatively normal life, until the parole period was over. In January 1957 he moved to Los Angeles on his own and got another job

# HE TOLD HER THE MAGAZINE NEEDED PICTURES OF A BOUND AND GAGGED GIRL

as a TV repairman. He found an apartment, bought a car and joined a photography club. It all seemed normal, as if he was putting his past behind him. Then he bought some expensive professional photography equipment and, posing as a photographer called Johnny Glynn, phoned a modelling agency saying he had a commission from a true crime magazine and needed a model. They put him in touch with Judy Dull, a nineteen-year-old model who had recently arrived in Los Angeles. He phoned her and asked her to come over to his studio, in reality his apartment. When she arrived he told her the magazine needed pictures of a bound and gagged girl. She allowed him to tie her up and he took photographs of her. Then he raped her, took her out into the desert, raped her again, strangled her and photographed her dead body.

Six months later he joined a lonely hearts club and, through it, met Shirley Bridgeford. On their one and only date, he picked her up from her house and, under the pretence of going for a drive and dinner out of town, he drove her into the desert. The same pattern occurred as before. He tied her up, raped her, strangled her with a piece of rope and took photographs of the process. He left her body in a remote area of the desert for the coyotes. The thrill lasted for four months this time, before he hired another model, Ruth Mercado. He used a different false name, but the result was the same.

The next few attempts he made failed when the models refused to accept his offers of work. Lorraine Vigil needed the money and accepted. Her agency warned her to be careful and, when he began to drive her out of Los Angeles, she protested. He pulled a gun on her but, unlike his other victims, she fought back. She managed to get out of the car and flag down a passing police patrol car. Glatman was arrested and, after extensive questioning, he confessed to the three murders. The detectives questioning him tricked him into revealing the location of the photographs and persuaded him to show them where the corpses of his victims were. Once they found the bodies, they had Glatman banged to rights. He fell to pieces, asking for the death sentence and recording a long, taped confession, admitting to every detail of his crimes and how he had planned them.

The trial was over quickly. The taped confession had a chilling effect on all those who heard it. If there had been any doubts about whether he was of sound mind or not, the tape removed them. He was found guilty of first-degree murder and sentenced to death. At 10am on 18 September 1959 he was strapped into a chair in the gas chamber in San Quentin State Prison. Sodium cyanide pellets where introduced into a solvent in the chamber, releasing cyanide gas, and, 12 minutes later, he was pronounced dead.

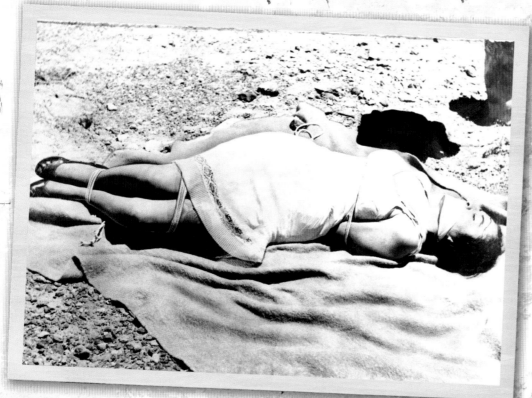

LEFT: The body of Ruth Mercado, photographed by Harvey Glatman.
OPPOSITE PAGE: Judy Dull posing for Harvey Glatman hours before her murder.

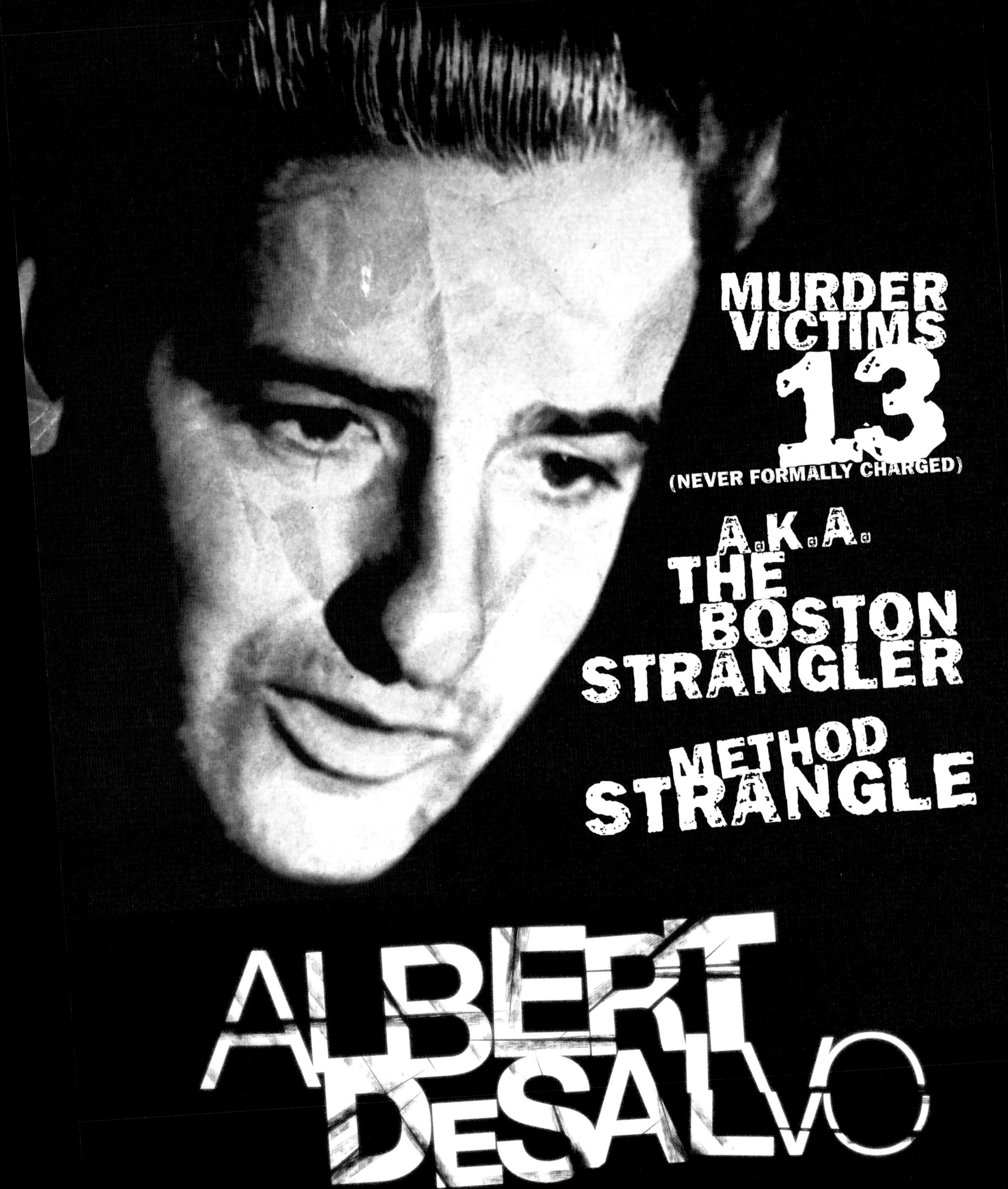

MURDER
VICTIMS
**13**
(NEVER FORMALLY CHARGED)

A.K.A.
THE
BOSTON
STRANGLER

METHOD
STRANGLE

ALBERT
DESALVO

**The Boston Strangler left his obscene signature on the women he murdered in the form of a bow elaborately tied around their throttled necks. Was this a clue to the killer's identity, or simply the fulfilment of some kind of sick fantasy? Until his capture in 1964 only Albert DeSalvo knew the answer.**

In an 18-month period, from June 1962 to January 1964, 11 women were raped and murdered in Boston. In almost every case a woman living on her own was sexually assaulted, strangled and left with the killer's 'signature' on them, an item of their own clothing tied in a bow around their necks. There was no sign of forced entry at the crime scenes. The killer either knew the victims, an unlikely scenario because of the number involved, or had talked his way into the women's apartments. Considering the avalanche of publicity the case attracted, the murdered women must have been aware of the danger of allowing a strange man into their homes. Whatever the killer said to persuade them to let him in, it must have been a very convincing story.

The first victim was Anna Slesers, a 55-year-old divorcee. On 14 June 1962 she was raped and strangled with the belt from her dressing gown. The belt was then tied around her neck and fashioned into a bow under her chin. Two weeks later Nina Nichols, 68, was killed in an almost identical way. The only difference was that the killer had used her stockings rather than a belt to strangle her. The time of death was established almost to the minute. At 5pm she had been talking to a friend on the phone when the door buzzer sounded. She said she'd ring straight back after she'd answered the door, but never did. Her body was found two hours later.

Two days later Helen Blake, who was 65, was reported missing. The police went to her apartment, where she lived alone, and found her lying face down on her bed. She had been strangled with her stockings, which were then tied around her neck in a bow. If there had been any doubt before, the police now knew for certain there was a maniac on the loose. With the police investigation apparently getting nowhere, the city was gripped by

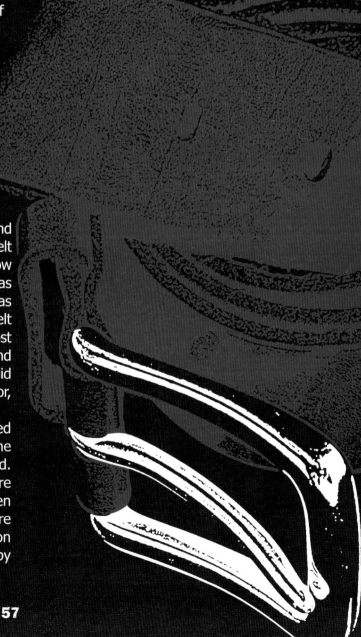

# THERE WAS A MANIAC ON THE LOOSE

panic. The newspapers found a name for the anonymous madman – the Boston Strangler.

Three weeks later, on 21 August, the 75-year-old widow Ida Irga was found in her apartment. Unlike the previous victims, she had been strangled by hand and a pillowcase had been knotted around her neck. But nobody was trying to pretend that she was not another victim of the Boston Strangler. It was obvious to all that the murder had been committed by the same man. At the end of August another body of an elderly woman was found in her apartment. She was 67-year-old Jane Sullivan and had been dead for more than a week, placing the time of her death very close to that of Ida Irga. On this occasion the killer had dragged the body into the bathroom after he had strangled her. She was left resting against the bath with her head underwater. The stockings used to strangle her were tied around her neck in the usual fashion.

And then nothing happened for three months. For the people of Boston, waiting in trepidation for the next attack, this was almost as bad as news of the attacks themselves. A Boston newspaper printed an appeal for the Boston Strangler to give himself up. They said he was a sick man and would be helped if he came in, but they got no response. Just when the public were beginning to believe the terror was over, the Strangler struck again. But, this time, he did something that serial killers

very rarely do. He changed the type of victim he chose to attack. Up until then all his victims were elderly or middle-aged women. This time he would attack a much younger one.

On 5 December 1962, twenty-year-old student Sophie Clark was murdered in the apartment she shared with two other students. She had been raped and strangled. Had it not been for the stocking tied in a bow around her neck, the police would not have attributed the murder to the Boston Strangler. As it was, they were not convinced the same man was involved in all the murders,

ABOVE: Mary Sullivan, victim of the Boston Strangler.

# *Flight of 'Strangler' Provides Rip-Roaring Story While It Lasts*

but, as far as the Boston public was concerned, the Strangler was back. On New Year's Eve another young woman, 23-year-old Patricia Bissette, was raped and strangled with her stockings.

No more attacks occurred until 8 May 1963, when another 23-year-old, Beverly Samans, was murdered. Unlike the previous victims, her hands had been tied behind her back before she was stabbed repeatedly in the throat and chest. Her killer then tied stockings and scarves around her neck. Was this another victim of the Boston Strangler or was someone trying to make it look that way? The Boston Police Department appeared clueless and the psychological profilers they had brought into the investigation were coming up with contradictory statements. The police even consulted a psychic, who told them the killer had a

scar on his left arm and loved shoes. It was not much help.

There was another four-month break and then another series of murders. The first victim was the 58-year-old divorcee Evelyn Corbin. The assault, carried out on 8 September 1963, bore all the hallmarks of a typical Boston Strangler attack, although the level of violence and sadism involved had increased. It appeared as if the strangler had reverted to his former choice of victim. But, in November and January of the following year, two more young women were raped and strangled. These attacks were more violent still.

By this time public confidence in the Boston Police Department's handling of the case had all but disappeared. The state police were called in and a special task force was set up to crack the case.

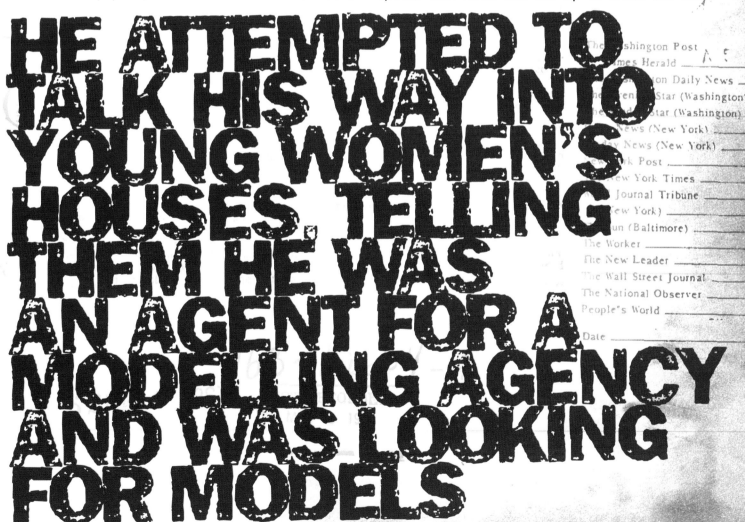

# HE ATTEMPTED TO TALK HIS WAY INTO YOUNG WOMEN'S HOUSES, TELLING THEM HE WAS AN AGENT FOR A MODELLING AGENCY AND WAS LOOKING FOR MODELS

# 'Boston Strangler Gives Up in Store'

ABOVE: Albert DeSalvo leaving Lynne Police Station.

RIGHT: Albert DeSalvo serving his sentence at Walpole State Prison, Massachusetts during the early 1970s.

Throughout the spring and summer of 1964 huge resources of manpower and money were poured into the investigation. Known sex offenders were interviewed, each case was gone over again and again, but still the investigation got nowhere. Time dragged on and, by October, ten months after the last attack, people were beginning to think the Boston Strangler had died, or moved away or just given up. On 27 October a young married woman was attacked in her apartment. She was tied up, indecently assaulted and then the attacker stopped before raping her, apologized and left. She gave a description to the police and they knew who it was straight away – Albert DeSalvo.

The police didn't suspect him as being the Boston Strangler. DeSalvo had served time for minor sexual assaults, but when his photograph was shown to rape victims in Massachusetts and then other states, there was an enormous rush of positive identifications. They had caught a serial rapist, who had committed more than 300 assaults. He was sent to a mental institution for psychological assessment and, while he was there, bragged to another inmate that he was the Boston Strangler. An attorney recorded a confession and handed it over to the police. In it he revealed knowledge of some details of the murders the police had not made public and admitted two other killings not previously attributed to the Boston Strangler. Rather than investigate DeSalvo further, he was put on trial for four of the sexual assaults out of the hundreds he had committed. He was convicted and sentenced to life imprisonment. On 26 November 1973 he was murdered in his prison cell, stabbed by an unknown assailant.

Albert DeSalvo certainly fits the profile of a serial killer. His father violently abused both his wife and their children, until she divorced him when

# Attorney Says DeSalvo Fears He'll Be Slain

DeSalvo was 13. At about this time he was beginning to commit petty crimes which would earn him several spells in young offenders' institutions. On the last occasion, after he was caught trying to steal a car, on his release, he joined the army. While serving in Germany he was court-martialled for the indecent assault of a nine-year-old girl, but the charges were dropped when her mother decided not to continue with the prosecution. By 1958, DeSalvo was out of the army and living in Boston with his wife and two children. He was working as a maintenance man, but was also breaking into houses. On a number of occasions over the next two years he attempted to talk his way into young women's houses, telling them he was an agent for a modelling agency and was looking for models. Once inside he would take the women's measurements, attempt to seduce them and, if that failed, leave. Until they caught him during a break-in, the police called him the Measuring Man and thought of him as being a nuisance to women rather than a danger. DeSalvo served ten months in prison for the break-in and, after his release, began his career as a serial rapist.

Although the progression from bothering women to raping them and then going on to kill them is typical of a serial killer, questions about the case continue to this day. The former FBI Agent Robert Ressler, who was a pioneer in the use of profiling in investigations and is often credited with introducing the term serial killer into public usage, has written that he believes there must have been more than one person responsible for all the murders. In his opinion there were too many differences in the behaviour patterns exhibited during the different murders to be able to pin them all on DeSalvo.

One of the extraordinary things about the case is that DeSalvo was not considered as a suspect at any point before he confessed. Some of the psychological profiles built up during the investigation were an almost perfect match for him and he had a history of sexual assault, so why wasn't he questioned about the Boston Strangler murders? And then, after he had confessed, why didn't the police investigate the claims he made in his confession? It is possible they were confident he would be found guilty on the rape charges so didn't charge him with crimes they were less sure about. The taped confession, in the absence of physical evidence, might not have been enough to secure a conviction. At least he would be off the streets and in prison if he was convicted of the rapes. Or, perhaps, they were trying to cover up a bungled investigation which should have identified DeSalvo at a much earlier point, saving the lives of some of his victims. In the absence of a full investigation it is impossible to get to the real story, or know for sure if Albert DeSalvo was definitely the Boston Strangler. Surely the victims and their families deserve better than that.

# MURDERS 5

## METHOD
TORTURE
STRANGLE
AXE

## VICTIMS YOUNG CHILDREN

# IAN BRADY &
# MYRA HINDLEY

**Ian Brady and Myra Hindley were devoted to one another – they were also devoted to the use of rape, torture and murder as a way of expressing and consummating their extraordinary relationship. For many the desolate beauty of Saddleworth Moor has come to represent the feelings of grief shared by local people for the young lives that were savagely wasted there so many years ago.**

Saddleworth Moor is in the Peak District National Park, about 16km (10 miles) north-east of Manchester. It can be a windswept and desolate place, but, as such places often are, it can be beautiful too. Since the arrest of Ian Brady and Myra Hindley, on 7 October 1966, it has come to be associated with the most infamous series of murders ever committed in Britain. The Moors Murderers, as they became known, buried four of their five victims on the moor and, despite extensive searches, the body of one of them has never been found. The nature of the crimes committed by Brady and Hindley were so heinous that, after they were caught, both were sentenced to serve a minimum life term of 30 years in prison. Myra Hindley, who was a heavy smoker, served 37 years before dying of a heart attack brought on by emphysema, and Ian Brady served 19 years in prison before being transferred to Broadmoor Hospital, a maximum-security psychiatric institution. Subsequently he was transferred again to Ashworth Hospital, a similar institution to Broadmoor, where he continues to be held.

Ian Brady and Myra Hindley met in 1961 while they were working for a chemical company in Manchester. Both had difficult childhoods, although for different reasons. Brady never knew his father and, while a teenager, was arrested on numerous occasions for burglary and assault. Hindley had been

# BRADY WAS OBSESSED WITH THE NAZI REGIME AND INTRODUCED HINDLEY TO SADOMASOCHISTIC SEX

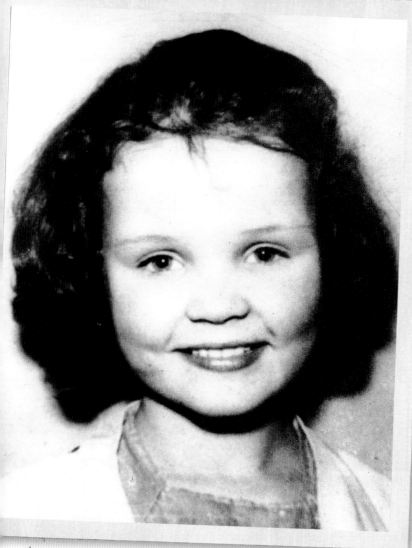

ABOVE: Portrait of Lesley Ann Downey, aged 10.

traumatized by the death of a close friend in a swimming accident when she was fifteen and had taken years to recover. Perhaps their troubled backgrounds encouraged a bond to develop between them. In the summer of 1962, Brady moved into the house Hindley shared with her infirm grandmother in Hattersley, on the outskirts of Manchester. Brady was four years older than Hindley and, initially at least, exerted an enormous influence over her. He was obsessed with the Nazi regime and introduced Hindley to sadomasochistic sex. Brady began to call her Myra Hess and she bleached her hair blonde at his request to make herself look more Germanic. Together they fantasized about committing crime. Brady was the dominant partner, but there can be no doubt that Hindley was his willing accomplice. On several occasions she attempted to leave him, but she always came back. Together they formed a partnership of a type known by the French term *folie à deux*, literally 'a madness of two', which can occur when two people share their lives to the exclusion of everybody and everything else. Brady and Hindley shared their fantasies and delusions, going on to commit appalling acts that, in all probability, neither would have contemplated on their own.

Initially Brady wanted to rob a bank. At some point in 1963, his fantasy changed. He wanted to commit the perfect murder. On 12 July Brady and Hindley decided on a plan. Hindley cruised the streets of Manchester in a van while Brady followed on his motorbike, looking out for a victim. He spotted Pauline Reade, a sixteen-year-old girl they both knew, and Hindley persuaded her to come up to the moors with the pretence of asking her to help look for a lost glove. Hindley drove to Saddleworth Moor with Pauline and Brady followed. While they were searching Brady attacked Pauline, hitting her over the head with a shovel. He raped her and cut her throat with a knife, almost decapitating her. Brady and Hindley buried the body in a shallow grave. Pauline Reade's body would not be recovered from the moor until 1987, when Hindley led police to the spot in an attempt to increase her chances of getting parole.

The next two killings were almost identical. Both victims, John Kilbride and Keith Bennett, were twelve years old and both were picked up by Hindley and taken up to the moor, one in November 1963 and the other in June 1964. Brady raped both boys and strangled them with a piece of string. Hindley claimed she stayed in the van for the first murder, but watched the second and took photographs. Brady has said she participated in both. The two of them then buried the bodies in shallow graves. Up until they were caught, Brady and Hindley returned to the moor regularly and took photographs of each other sitting by the graves. These photographs would enable the police to find

John Kilbride's body shortly after Brady and Hindley were arrested. Keith Bennett's body has never been found, despite intensive searches of the moor. Brady has said he knows were it is, but has, so far, refused to divulge the information, causing great distress to the victim's family.

On Boxing Day 1964, Brady and Hindley abducted ten-year-old Lesley Ann Downey after she became separated from her family at a fairground. They took her back to their house in Hattersley and forced her to strip while they took pornographic photographs of her. Both of them tortured her over a period of several hours, then raped her before finally strangling her with a piece of string. While they were doing this, they recorded her screaming and begging for her life on audio tape. The following day, they took the body up to the moor and buried it. The depravity of this crime in particular, together with the callous attitudes Brady and Hindley showed after they were caught, is what has made them the most reviled and hated

THEY RECORDED HER SCREAMING AND BEGGING FOR HER LIFE ON AUDIO TAPE

murderers in British history. The tape and photographs of Lesley Ann Downey were among the principal items of evidence used to convict the two of them. The tape was so harrowing it is said to have reduced experienced police officers who listened to it to tears. It also showed that Hindley was more than just an accomplice. Her voice can clearly be heard on the tape encouraging Brady and taunting the little girl.

For their next murder they attempted to get David Smith, Hindley's seventeen-year-old brother-in-law, involved. On 6 October 1965 Brady met Edward Evans, who was also seventeen, and persuaded him to come to the house. Hindley, meanwhile, invited Smith over to have a drink with her. Smith was in the kitchen when the screaming began. On going into the living room, he found Edward Evans in a chair and Brady standing over him, hitting him repeatedly with a hand axe. Brady handed the axe to the stunned Smith and strangled Evans to make sure he was dead. In fear of his life, Smith then helped Brady and Hindley carry the body upstairs to one of the bedrooms and then

clean-up the living room. After listening to Brady and Hindley discussing the murder and their previous crimes, Smith went home to his wife and told her what had happened. They went to a phone box, armed with a kitchen knife in case Brady came after them, and called the police.

Brady was arrested the next morning after police searched the house. They found Evans's body in the bedroom with the murder weapon next to it in a paper bag. Brady confessed to the murder and implicated Smith, but said Hindley knew nothing about it. A young girl who lived nearby told the police that Brady and Hindley had taken her to Saddleworth Moor in December 1964. She showed them the spot and a search began, involving hundreds of volunteers as well as police officers. The bodies of Lesley Ann Downey and John Kilbride were recovered. The police continued to search the house in Hattersley and found tickets for the left luggage office in Manchester Central Station hidden in the spine of a book. They recovered suitcases containing a wealth

# TWO SADISTIC KILLERS OF THE UTMOST DEPRAVITY

of incriminating evidence, including the photographs and tape of Lesley Ann Downey. Five days after Brady's arrest, Hindley was also arrested, by which time she had disposed of some evidence, but the contents of the suitcases where more than enough.

Brady and Hindley were put on trial at Chester Assizes in April 1966 for the murder of the three children whose bodies had been found. Both denied all charges at first and attempted to blame David Smith for the murder of Edward Evans. While they were in custody both had to be protected from other inmates and they were surrounded by bulletproof glass in the courtroom while the trial continued. They maintained a look of studied indifference, even when the tape of Lesley Ann Downey was played to the court. Brady was found guilty on all charges and Hindley of two murders and one count of accessory to murder. In his summing up, the judge described them as 'two sadistic killers of the utmost depravity'. He went on to say that he didn't think Brady could ever be reformed, but there was a chance for Hindley once she had been removed from Brady's influence.

In 1967, a year after Hindley had been sentenced, she asked Lord Longford to visit her in prison. At the time he was the leader of the House of Lords and was a noted author and social reformer. For many years he had been going on prison visits and campaigning on issues of prison reform and the rehabilitation of offenders. He was also deeply religious, having converted to Catholicism in his youth, and took his religious convictions very seriously, particularly those concerning forgiveness and redemption. For many years he visited Hindley in prison and argued that she should be treated in the same way as any other prisoner, which included allowing her the possibility of parole. Hindley convinced him she had returned to the Catholic church and had confessed to all her crimes. Taking her at her word, Longford mounted a vigorous campaign to get her released. He was viciously derided and lampooned in the press for, as they saw it, coming under Hindley's evil spell. They called him a silly old man and Lord Wrongford. In 1986 Hindley finally confessed in full to her part in all the murders, including the two she had not been charged with, believing it would help her case for parole. It confirmed she had been lying to Longford all along. In the following years successive home secretaries consistently denied her appeals, which continued up until her death in 2002. Ian Brady, on the other hand, appears to have accepted he will never be released and will die in Ashworth Hospital.

# WANTED

SAN FRANCISCO POLICE DEPARTMENT

IDENTIFIED MURDERS 5

CLAIMED MURDERS 37

METHOD SHOOTING STABBING

# ZODIAC KILLER

**The self-named Zodiac Killer seemed to murder for publicity alone. He was the twisted mastermind and press officer for a one-man campaign of terror on the streets of San Francisco during the late 1960s and early 1970s. Despite all his compulsive attention-seeking, his true identity remains a mystery.**

The series of unsolved murders in and around the San Francisco Bay area during the late 1960s and early 1970s has prompted more media attention and amateur attempts to identify the murderer than any other case of its kind since Jack the Ripper. The killer courted publicity and was described by a number of witnesses and victims who survived, but the extensive police investigation failed to identify him. It was almost as if the purpose of the murders was to attract attention to himself. He appeared to kill for the publicity alone.

After the first two attacks, the killer began to write a series of letters and make phone calls to the police and journalists in San Francisco, giving details only the real murderer could have known. He used the name 'the Zodiac' and always included a symbol of a circle with a cross over it in each letter. It looked like the sights of a rifle, but could also have represented the wheel of the zodiac. The letters and phone calls taunted the San Francisco Police Department about their inability to catch him and, on four occasions, included coded messages in the letters which, the Zodiac said, once deciphered, would reveal his identity.

The first attack was on 20 December 1968. Two teenagers, David Faraday and Betty Lou Jensen, parked their car in a secluded spot near the Lake Herman reservoir, above Vallejo in the San Francisco Bay Area. A witness later said he had seen two cars parked there, but had thought nothing of it at the time. David Faraday was shot in the head from close range as he sat in the car and died later in hospital. Betty Lou Jensen was shot five times in the back as she tried to run from the killer and died at the scene.

Just over six months later, on

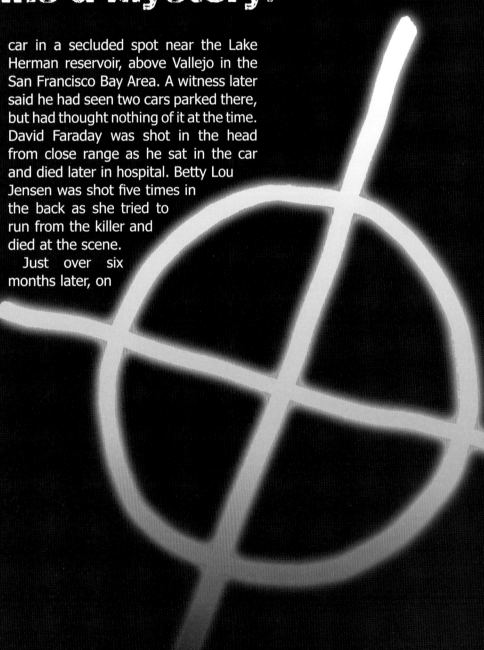

October 26, 1970

# FORTY YEARS OLD STOCKILY BUILT AND HAD BROWN HAIR

4 July 1969, Darlene Ferrin, a married woman of 22, and 19-year-old Michael Mageau were both shot while they sat in a car in the Blue Rock Springs Golf Course car park. It was another quiet spot frequently used by couples, about 6 km (4 miles) from the scene of the first shooting. Another car drove into the car park and stopped immediately behind their car. A man got out and shined a torch in their faces, then began shooting with a 9 mm handgun. Despite being hit in the face, neck and chest, Michael Mageau survived and was able to give the police a description of the shooter. Darlene Ferrin was hit nine times and was pronounced dead when her body arrived at a local hospital.

A man phoned the Vallejo Police Department shortly after the shooting to claim responsibility for the murder and for the earlier killing of Betty Lou Jensen. The call was traced to a phone box over the road from the sheriff's office and within sight of Darlene Ferrin's house. A witness had seen a man using the phone box at about the right time and gave a description. During the police investigation it emerged that Darlene Ferrin may have known the man who killed her. A white car was seen outside her house on a number of occasions, and a babysitter in Ferrin's house got a good view of the man in the car. Her description of him was similar to those given by other witnesses. He was about forty years old, stockily built and had brown hair. Unsubstantiated rumours began to circulate suggesting Darlene had seen this man commit a murder and was blackmailing him, but nothing came of the investigation.

Shortly afterwards, letters apparently sent by the man responsible for the murders arrived at the offices of three different newspapers in San Francisco. The writer, calling himself the Zodiac, included the symbol of a circle with a cross over it and claimed credit for the attacks. The letters also included the first of the ciphers, which the Zodiac wanted published on the front page of the papers. He said if it was not printed he would go on a killing rampage, not stopping until he had murdered 12 people. Military code breaking experts failed to crack the code, but a couple of school teachers succeeded. It included a number of mistakes and a jumble of letters at the end which are, apparently, nonsense, but did not contain his name. It read:

I like killing people because it is so much fun it is more fun than killing wild game in the forest because man is the most dangerous animal of all to kill something gives me the most thrilling experience it is even better that getting your rocks off with a girl the best part of it is that when I die I will be reborn in paradice and all the people I have killed will become my slaves I will not give you my name because you will try to sloi down or stop my collecting for my afterlife EBEORIET EMETH HPITI

Another young couple, Brian Hartnell and Cecelia Shepard, were attacked on 27 September 1969 while they were picnicking by a lake in the Napa Valley, about 32 km (20 miles) north of Vallejo. They were approached by a man wielding a gun who was wearing a hood which had the Zodiac symbol on it. He told them he was an escaped convict and needed their car. Both were tied up and and stabbed multiple times. The man then wrote in felt tip pen on the door of the couple's car, giving the dates of his previous attacks and drawing the zodiac symbol before casually walking away. Brian Hartnell somehow survived, but Cecelia Shepard died two days later in hospital. An hour after the stabbings, the killer phoned the police to report the crime and to tell them he had left a message at the scene to prove he really was the Zodiac. The call was traced to a pay phone in Napa, where the police found a palm print and a trail of footprints, but the investigation got no further.

The last murder that can definitely be attributed to the Zodiac was of the San Francisco taxi driver Paul Stine, on 11 October 1969. He was shot in the head by the passenger of his cab. Ballistic tests on the bullet showed the gun was the same one used to shoot David Faraday and Betty Lou Jensen. There were a number of witnesses who called the police while the incident was in progress. They watched the man take Stine's wallet and keys, rip a piece of cloth from Stine's shirt, wipe the inside of the cab down with it and calmly walk away. The police arrived on the scene within minutes. One police officer

TO: Sgt.

FROM:

RE: Zodiac strike dates

If Zodiac continued they should have f...

| MONTH | PISCES ... |
| --- | --- |
| Nov. | |
| Dec. | |
| Jan. | 10-11 (Sat |
| Feb. | 6-7 (Fri-S |
| March | 6-7 (Fri-S |
| April | 1-2 (Wed-Thur) |
| May | 1 (Fri) 27-28 ( |
| June | 23-24 (Tue |
| July | 20-21 (Mon |
| Aug. | 17-18 (Mon |
| Sept. | 13-14 (Sun |
| Oct. | 11-12 (Sun |
| Nov. | 7-8 (Sat |
| Dec. | 4-5 (Fri-S |
| Jan. | 1-2 (Fri-Sat) 28- |
| Feb. | 24-25 (Wed |
| Mar | 24-25 (Wed |
| Apr | 20-21 (Tue |
| May | 18-19 (Tue |
| | 14-15 (Mon |
| Jul | 11-12 (Sun- |
| | 7-8 (Sat-S |
| | 5 (Sat-Su |
| | (-Sat) 29-30 |
| Nov | 25-26 (Thur |
| | 22-23 (Wed |

HE WOULD GO ON A KILLING RAMPAGE, NOT STOPPING UNTIL HE HAD MURDERED TWELVE PEOPLE

even saw a man walking away from the scene, but didn't stop him because the description of the suspect given out by the police radio dispatcher had been the wrong one.

A few days later a letter from the Zodiac arrived at the offices of the *San Francisco Chronicle*. It included a piece of the cloth from Paul Stine's shirt to prove it was authentic. It was only then that the police realized how close they had come to catching the Zodiac. In the letter he bragged about chatting to some cops just before he had taken the cab and threatened to start shooting children on school buses. This was the first of a barrage of phone calls and letters from the Zodiac. They included three more ciphers, none of which have ever been decoded, and various threats, including one claiming he had built a bomb which he intended to plant on a school bus.

On 22 October a man claiming to be the Zodiac phoned the police to demand they put him in touch with Melvin Belli, one of America's most prominent lawyers. He said he would call a radio phone-in show the next day and wanted Belli to be there to take the call. Belli agreed to talk to the man and, the following day, had a long conversation with him. Police later traced the call to a mental institution and proved it was a hoax, although Belli received a Christmas card that year containing a message from the Zodiac and another piece of Paul Stine's shirt. The message said the Zodiac wanted to be helped but something in his head was stopping him. He said if he was not helped he would lose control again and take his ninth and tenth victims.

After March 1971 no more genuine letters arrived. Unsolved murders continued to

# Zodiac: 4 years later

## What happened to the killer who kept The City in terror?

BELOW: Handwritten note from the Zodiac Killer, boasting that he has now killed seven people.

occur in the San Francisco Bay Area, but none of them could definitely be attributed to the Zodiac. In January 1974 the Zodiac broke his silence. He wrote to the *San Francisco Chronicle*. The letter ended with the message 'Me = 37, SFPD = 0', obviously implying the Zodiac was keeping score, claiming to have killed a total of 37 people while the police had come up with nothing. Then there was a silence of four years before another genuine letter arrived. It announced that the Zodiac was back, but also said *'I am in control of all things'*. After that there were no more murders and no more contact from the Zodiac. The police speculated he had either been in prison or in a mental institution during the four-year silence, but no further progress was made in identifying him.

There have been a huge number of hoaxes and even some copycat killings since, but the Zodiac has maintained his silence. Theories about his identity abound, ranging from the plausible to the absurd. In 1986 Robert Graysmith, who had been a cartoonist on the *San Francisco Chronicle* and had taken an avid interest in the case right from the beginning, published a book on the Zodiac killings. In it he accused a man of being the killer, giving him the pseudonym Robert Hall Starr. The man had been a principal suspect in the police investigation and had been committed to a mental institution from 1974 to 1978 after he had molested a child, but no definite proof of his guilt was ever established.

The Hollywood film *Zodiac*, released in 2007 and starring Jake Gyllenhaal, Robert Downey Jr. and Mark Ruffalo, was based on Graysmith's book. It identified the same man as the killer, but used his real name rather than the pseudonym given in the book. The man died in 1992, allowing the film to name him without the producers being sued for libel. In 2002, DNA testing on the Zodiac letters indicated the man named in the film was not the same man who wrote the letters. The police file on the Zodiac killings remains open.

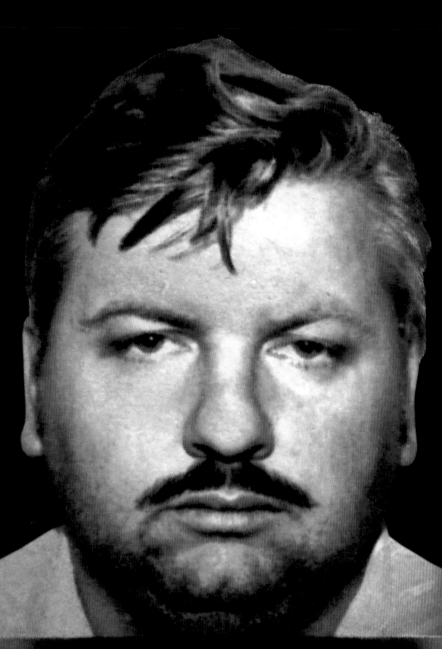

MURDERS
**33**

METHOD
STRANGLE

EXECUTION
LETHAL
INJECTION

POLICE DEPT.

JOHN WAYNE GACY

John Wayne Gacy was a successful businessman, charity worker and children's entertainer, but as his alter ego 'Bad Jack', he cruised the streets at night looking for boys to attack and kill. By the time police finally tracked him down, 'Bad Jack' had had his way with 33 boys and young men, but was Gacy really mad, or just really bad?

At his trial in 1979 for the murder of 33 boys and young men, John Wayne Gacy entered a plea of insanity. He claimed to have multiple personalities. There was the successful Chicago businessman who ran his own construction company; the political worker, who raised money for the Democrats and had met and been photographed with the First Lady, Rosalyn Carter, the wife of President Jimmy Carter; and the charity fundraiser who organized parties for underprivileged children, where he would dress up as Pogo the Clown to entertain them. Then there was Bad Jack. Bad Jack prowled the streets of Chicago at night looking for boys to pick up. He took them back to his house where he tortured and raped them. Then he strangled them and either dumped their bodies in the crawl space under the house, buried them in the grounds, or threw them in the Des Plaines river. Gacy confessed to the murders after his arrest, so the defence case rested on the insanity plea. Gacy's attorney asked the court if they thought a sane man would live in a house under which there were 28 decomposing bodies.

There is a depressing familiarity about Gacy's childhood. He was born in Chicago in 1942 and was named by his parents, Stanley and Marion Gacy, after their favourite movie star. As a child he was nothing like his

# HE WAS OVERWEIGHT, OFTEN UNWELL AND QUITE EFFEMINATE

namesake. He was overweight, often unwell and quite effeminate. His father, an abusive alcoholic, called him a sissy and beat him often, no doubt telling his son he would whip him into shape. Marion Gacy and his two older sisters dominated Gacy, constantly taunting him and treating him as the baby of the family even as he grew into his late teens. It would lead to a suppressed hatred for women that would last for the rest of his life.

In 1964, at the age of 22, Gacy married Marilyn Myer, who he met in the shoe store where he worked as a salesman. The couple moved to Waterloo, Iowa, where Meyer was from, and her father gave Gacy a job managing the Kentucky Fried Chicken franchise he owned there. They had two children and Gacy joined the Jaycees – a civic organisation which did good works in the community. Gacy appeared to be a model citizen, but rumours about his personal life, specifically his relationships with teenage boys, were

already circulating. In 1968 he was arrested for the sexual assault of a minor. The father of a fifteen-year-old boy, known to Gacy, had made a complaint about him to the police. Gacy was convicted and given the maximum sentence for the charges, ten years in prison. Inexplicably, he served just 18 months before being paroled.

While Gacy was in prison his wife divorced him, saying she never wanted to see him again. After he was released he returned to Chicago, and he appeared to be trying to put his past behind him. He started his own construction company, bought a big house in Norwood Park, a north Chicago suburb, joined the Democratic party and got married again. But, underneath this veneer of respectability, his sexual tastes had taken an even darker turn. Unknown to his wife, Gacy was hanging around the area of Chicago known as Bughouse Square trying to pick up rent boys and teenage runaways.

The first time he murdered one of the boys he picked up was, according to his confession, in January 1972. His wife was out of town and Gacy made the most of the opportunity to bring the boy back to the house in Norwood Park. He asphyxiated the boy with a rope while they were having sex. Eventually Gacy strangled the boy to death and dumped the body through a hidden trap door in a closet into the crawl space below the house. The boy, like so many of Gacy's victims, remains unidentified. After his arrest, Gacy said he only knew the first names of most of his victims and couldn't remember which was which.

From then on, every time Gacy's wife went out of town, he would go out looking for more victims. In 1976 his wife found homosexual pornography in the house. When she confronted Gacy with it, he admitted he preferred young boys to women. She left him and began divorce proceedings. After his wife had gone, Gacy was not so constrained about how often he could bring boys back to the house. The number of murders snowballed. As well as picking them up in Bughouse Square Gacy began to employ boys in temporary labouring jobs with his construction company, he would then try to lure them back to his house. In 1976 seventeen-year-old Johnny Butkovich, Michael Bonnin, also seventeen, and Billy Carroll, sixteen, all went missing within a few months of each other. They had all worked for Gacy at different times. It seems incredible now that the Chicago police didn't make the connection. Over the course of the following year three more boys known to Gacy also went missing. It emerged at his trial that Gacy, after luring boys into his house, would ask them if they wanted to see a trick with handcuffs. He put the handcuffs on the boys

and told them the trick was to have the keys. Then he sexually assaulted and murdered them.

Jeffrey Ringall didn't fit the general profile of Gacy's victims. He was 27 years old and lived with his girlfriend in Chicago. On 22 May 1978, Ringall was walking through the New Town district when a heavy-set man in a black Oldsmobile pulled over and offered him a lift. Ringall accepted and got into the car. The man was John Wayne Gacy and, during the ride, he leant over to Ringall and held a chloroform-soaked rag over his face, quickly rendering Ringall unconscious. Gacy drove back to his house and carried Ringall up to the bedroom. When Ringall regained consciousness he was tied to a rack. Gacy spent the next few hours subjecting Ringall to an ordeal of rape and torture,

OPPOSITE PAGE: John Wayne Gacy, shown here at his wedding with his second wife, Carole Hoff, in June 1972.
BELOW: Police use a ground penetrating radar device to search for bodies behind an apartment building on Chicago's Northwest Side, following reports that Gacy carried out some late-night construction work on the building.

# POLICE FOUND THE HIDDEN TRAP DOOR AND DECOMPOSING HUMAN REMAINS BELOW IT

before knocking him out with chloroform again.

For some unknown reason Gacy didn't kill Ringall. He dumped the unconscious young man in Lincoln Park in central Chicago. When he woke up the next morning Ringall went to a hospital, where he spent the next six days recovering from the injuries he had sustained at Gacy's hands. He reported the assault to the Chicago police, but as he couldn't remember very much of what had happened, the investigation didn't get very far, but Ringall was not prepared to let it drop. One of the few things he could remember was regaining consciousness for a few seconds during the drive to Gacy's house. Before being drugged again, he recognized the exit from the highway they were taking. On his own initiative, Ringall decided to watch the exit to see if his attacker would take the same route again. Within hours of parking his car within sight of the exit, Ringall saw the black Oldsmobile. He

followed it to a house in Norwood Park. It took him a while to find out who owned the house, but, when he did, Ringall went back to the police. By that time an investigation into John Wayne Gacy had already begun.

In December 1978 fifteen-year-old Robert Piest went missing. He didn't show up after arranging to meet his mother and she rang the police. The last thing he had said to her was that he was going to see a man about a construction job. The police established that the man was John Wayne Gacy. They went to his house without a search warrant, because they didn't have enough evidence against him to get one, and found a receipt made out in the name of a girl known to Piest. The receipt was for a roll of film the girl had asked Piest to drop off at a shop to be developed. Gacy tried to call their bluff and, when the police began a surveillance operation, filed a lawsuit against them citing an illegal search of his property and police harassment. But, by this time, details of his previous sexual offence in Iowa had come to light and a search warrant was issued.

The first thing the police officers conducting the search noticed was the terrible smell in the house, which Gacy said was due to a problem with the drains. Then they found the hidden trap door in the closet. One of the officers opened it and was almost overcome by the stench of decomposing human remains. Gacy was arrested and the grisly task of recovering and identifying the remains began. Despite extensive and painstaking work, only 12 of the 33 victims could be named. The remaining 21 were buried as John Does. In the years since their discovery, only two of the unknown boys have been formally identified.

At Gacy's trial evidence was given by people who had been attacked by him, but not killed, one of them was Jeffrey Ringall. He was clearly still traumatized by his ordeal, but he managed to give an account of what

Gacy had put him through. Everything pointed towards premeditated murder. One psychiatrist testifying for the defence suggested Gacy suffered from episodes of temporary insanity while he was committing the murders, but then recovered enough to dispose of the bodies. The prosecution asked if he could have been temporarily insane on 33 separate occasions. The defence, realizing they were not convincing anyone of Gacy's insanity, changed tack. They suggested Gacy had accidentally killed all 33 boys by asphyxiating them during consensual sex.

The jury dismissed the insanity plea and were not impressed with the defence claim of accidental death. Gacy was found guilty on all counts of first-degree murder. He was sentenced to death and spent the next 14 years on death row while an exhaustive appeals process was carried out. Then, on 10 May 1994, after the final appeal had failed, he was sent to the execution chamber in Stateville Correctional Center in Crest Hill, Illinois, where he was executed by lethal injection. At no point during the entire time of his trial or while he was in prison, did Gacy express any remorse for his actions. His last words were reportedly to one of the prison guards leading him to his execution, he said *'You can kiss my ass'.*

OPPOSITE PAGE: Richard and Rosemary Szyc holding a framed picture of their son John, who was murdered by John Wayne Gacy in 1977.
BELOW: A selection of some of the 5,000 demonstrators who marched in the Gacy Day Parade in support of the execution of John Wayne Gacy in Chicago on 9 May 1994.

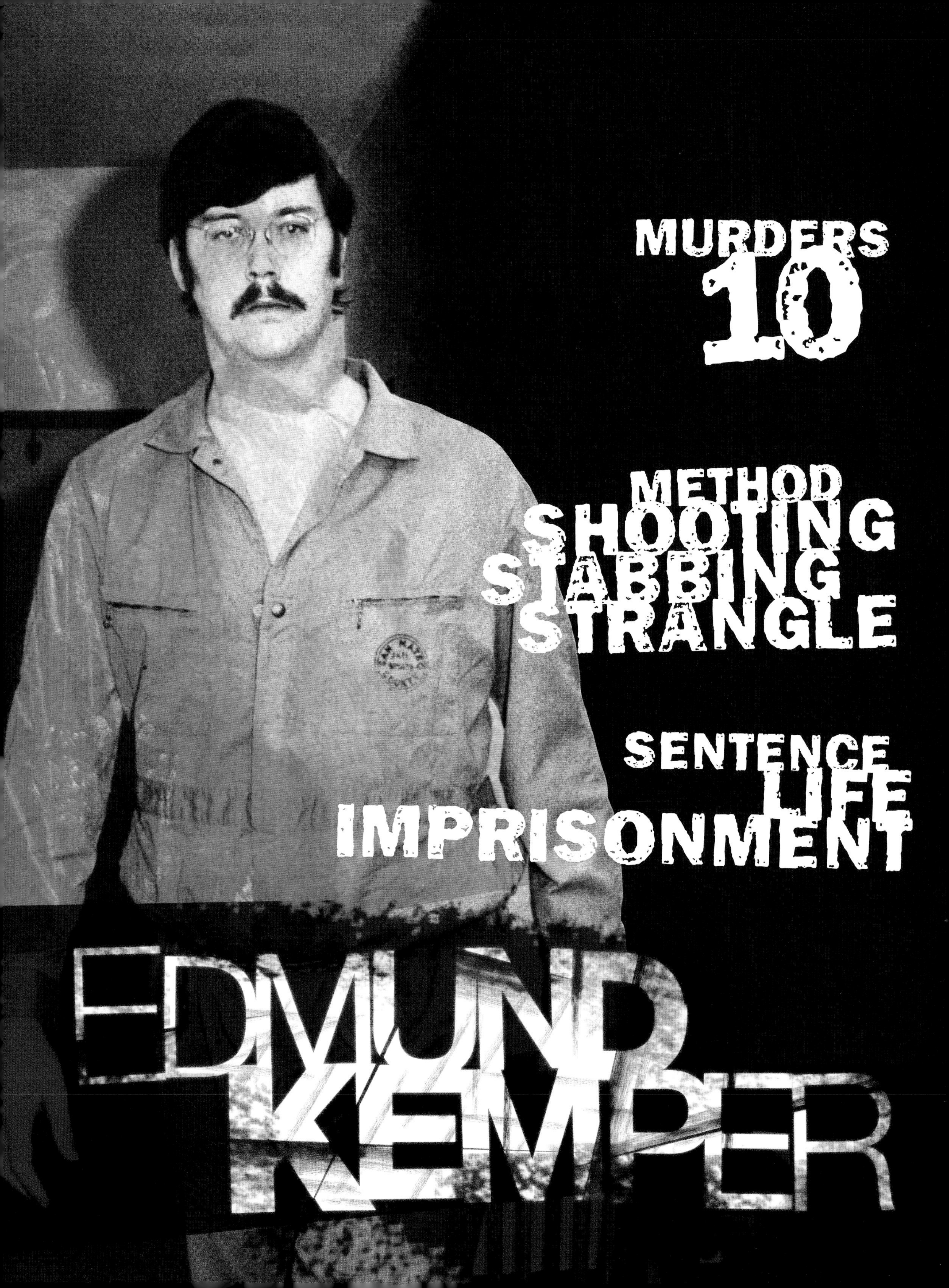

MURDERS
**10**

METHOD
SHOOTING
STABBING
STRANGLE

SENTENCE
LIFE
IMPRISONMENT

EDMUND KEMPER

**Ed Kemper was a personal friend of the LAPD, hanging out in cop bars where he could follow the police investigation into a spate of gruesome attacks on young female hitch-hikers. Little did the LAPD know that the killer was sitting right under their noses the whole time, and he'd been using their inside information to avoid capture and to keep on killing.**

Santa Cruz, a city on the Californian coast about 112 km (70 miles) south of San Francisco, felt like a dangerous place to live early in 1973. There were a string of murders in the city and the surrounding area, which the police attributed to two separate serial killers. The local newspapers were hardly making life any easier. They printed lurid stories, inventing details to make the murders even worse than they already were, and called the city the 'murder capital of America'. The police department was under pressure and was being criticized from all sides. Off-duty officers in the Jury Room, a cop bar in the city, talked over the details of the case. Edmund Kemper liked to hang around the bar, talking to the cops. They called him Big Ed because of his size, he was 6 ft 9 in (2 m 6 cm) and heavily built, and wanted to be a cop himself. He had applied to join the department, but they said he was too big. He got on well with the cops and one of them had given him a pair of handcuffs.

In February 1973 the police in Santa Cruz caught Herbert Mullin after he had killed for the thirteenth time. No doubt the cops in the Jury Room celebrated with a few drinks, but they knew they still had another one to catch – the man the newspapers were calling the Co-ed Killer, because the victims were all female hitchhikers and most of them were students. The cops told Big Ed about the case, giving him details of how the investigation was going. Two months

later Kemper phoned the police from Pueblo, Colorado, to turn himself in. He said he had killed his mother and another woman and confessed to being the Co-ed Killer. They didn't believe him at first, until officers went to look in the apartment he shared with his mother.

Edmund Kemper was a strange child. His mother once found the remains of the family's pet in his bedroom. He had killed it, mutilated its body and cut

ABOVE: Portrait of Aito Koo, victim of Edmund Kemper.

OPPOSITE PAGE: A police officer removes the manacles from Edmund Kemper's wrists prior to the reading of the verdict in Kemper's trial for the murders of eight women.

its head off. After his parents divorced and subsequently remarried, his behaviour became worse. Some nights his mother locked him in the basement because she was afraid he would attack his sisters. In the summer of 1964, when he was fifteen, he was sent to stay with his grandparents in the Sierra Mountains. Maybe, his parents thought, living an outdoor lifestyle would straighten him out. On 27 August he shot and killed his grandmother as she sat at the kitchen table while his grandfather was out. When he came back, Kemper shot his grandfather too. He then phoned the police to tell them what he had done. When asked why he had killed them, he said 'To see what it felt like to kill grandma'.

Kemper spent the next five years in a hospital for the criminally insane. While there he took an interest in psychiatry and learned to tell his doctors exactly what they wanted to hear. Although diagnosed as a paranoid schizophrenic, in 1969 he was released into his mother's custody. While they were living together, the pair of them were always arguing. Nothing Kemper could do was ever good enough for her. Eventually he found an apartment in Alameda, near San Francisco, and moved out.

In the early 1970s college students were often hitchhiking along the California coast. At first Kemper picked up girls just to talk to them. He kept a gun in the car and fantasized about what he would do to them. On 7 May 1972 he crossed the line between fantasy and reality. Mary Ann Pesce and Anita Luchessa were both eighteen-year-old co-eds. Kemper picked them up near Stanford University and pulled the gun on them. He forced Anita Luchessa into the trunk of his car and handcuffed Mary Ann Pesce, before putting a plastic bag over her head and strangling her. She tried to fight back, so he stabbed her and then cut her throat. Then he opened to the trunk and stabbed Anita Luchessa, and, when she was dead, he took the two bodies back to his apartment. Once there he cut their heads off and dismembered the bodies. He buried the remains in a

# WHEN ASKED WHY HE HAD KILLED THEM, HE SAID 'TO SEE WHAT IT FELT LIKE TO KILL GRANDMA'

# HIS MOTHER ONCE FOUND THE REMAINS OF THE FAMILY'S PET IN HIS BEDROOM. HE HAD KILLED IT, MUTILATED ITS BODY AND CUT ITS HEAD OFF

remote spot in the mountains, except for the heads, which he kept for some time before throwing them into a ravine.

The next victim was fifteen-year-old Aito Koo. On 14 September Kemper picked her up hitchhiking and drove up into the mountains, where he raped and strangled her. He dismembered the body and buried the remains, keeping the head, as he had before. The next day it was in the trunk of his car when he attended a court hearing to establish if he was now sufficiently rehabilitated for his juvenile record to be sealed. Incredibly the court were convinced enough to decide in his favour.

In January and February Kemper killed three more hitchhikers. Body parts were beginning to show up and the cops in the Jury Room were talking to Big Ed about it. By this time he had moved back to his mother's place. They were still arguing all the time and, on 5 April, Kemper decided to solve the problem once and for all. He hit her over the head with a hammer while she was sleeping and cut her head off. Then he cut out her vocal cords and threw them into the waste disposal unit. There would be no more arguments with his mother, but he was not finished yet. He phoned Sally Hallet, a friend of his mother's, and invited her over for dinner. As soon as she arrived, he strangled her and raped the body. The next morning he got in his car and drove away. He kept driving until he got to Pueblo, where he stopped and made the call to the police.

At his trial on eight counts of murder Kemper confessed to necrophilia and cannibalism, although these details may have been an attempt to bolster the plea of insanity he had entered. He was found guilty and asked for the death penalty. Capital punishment had been suspended in the State of California at the time and he was sentenced to life imprisonment.

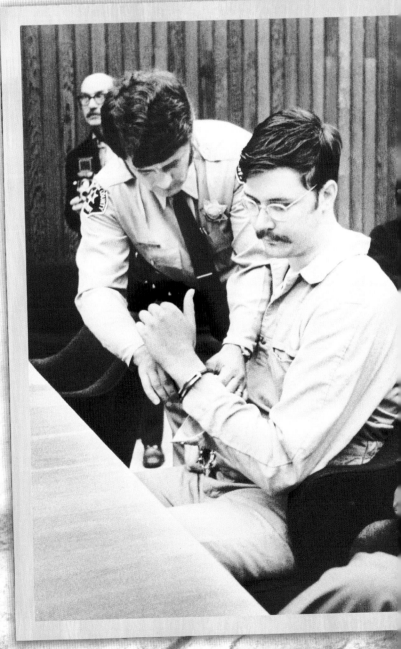

MURDER COUNT **30**

VICTIMS **YOUNG WOMEN**

METHOD **BLUDGEON STRANGLE RAPE**

# TED BUNDY

**Ted Bundy achieved celebrity status in the US as a vicious killer of young women. Strangely, women and girls flocked to his trial like moths to a flame, eager to hear all about the depraved crimes he'd committed as if he were a performing rock star or a sex symbol. Undoubtedly the families of his many victims weren't nearly as star-struck, and were relieved to see justice served once and for all.**

At his trial in Dade County, Florida, in June 1979, Ted Bundy conducted his own defence. It was one of the first trials in America to be extensively televised and Bundy played to the gallery. It was as if he was appearing in a TV courtroom drama rather than on trial for his life. Although he had studied law, he had dropped out before finishing the degree. Even so, he was confident and articulate in the courtroom. At one stage he used an obscure loophole in Florida law to get married to his girlfriend while she was on the stand giving evidence. The trial gripped America and Bundy attracted a large female following. They were, apparently, fascinated by the man accused of committing appalling crimes against other women. But the act didn't fool everyone – to some people he came across as calculating and manipulative. The forensic evidence against him was compelling, particularly the comparison of bite marks found on one of his victims and a plaster cast taken of his teeth. The jury pronounced him guilty of first-degree murder. In his closing remarks, the judge told Bundy he would have made a good lawyer if he had chosen a different path and, bizarrely, that he should take care of himself. Seconds before, the judge had also told him he would be put to death in the electric chair.

Bundy was born in a home for unwed mothers in 1946 and was initially brought up by his grandparents,

thinking that his real mother, Louise Cowell, was his sister. Years later he found out the truth, that she was actually his mother, and the shock of the discovery is said to have had a major psychological affect on him. The identity of his father is unknown, although allegations have been made of incest against his grandfather. In 1951 Louise and Ted Cowell moved to Tacoma, Washington, and inexplicably changed their surnames from Cowell to Nelson. It was as if they were trying to leave their former lives behind. A year after arriving in Tacoma, Louise married John Bundy. Ted adopted his stepfather's name and would keep it for the rest of his life, although

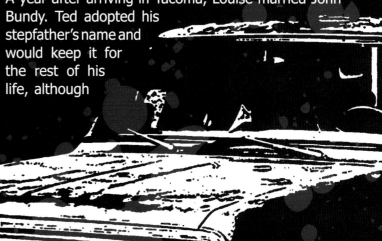

he later said the relationship between them was distant and difficult. The family grew with the addition of four children and, in his teenage years, Ted Bundy would often babysit his stepbrothers and stepsisters.

As Bundy grew up he became obsessed with violent pornography and images of sadistic sex. He became a compulsive shoplifter and began to creep around the neighbourhood at night, peeping into women's bedrooms and fantasizing about what he could do to them. Despite this aberrant behaviour, he was a good student, doing well enough to be accepted by the University of Washington in Seattle in 1965 to study psychology. While he was there he met his first serious girlfriend, but the relationship didn't survive after she left college. Over the next few years he wrote to her obsessively, wanting to get back together, but she had moved on and considered him to be too immature for her. Many of his future victims would bear a striking resemblance to her.

Detectives and FBI profilers who interviewed Bundy after his arrest believed he had started killing years before he admitted he had in a series of confessions. The first attack that can definitely be attributed to him was on 4 January 1974. He broke into the apartment shared by Susan Clark, an eighteen-year-old University of Washington student, and two other students and attacked her while she was sleeping. He sexually assaulted her and beat her over the head with a metal bar, fracturing her skull, but, miraculously, she survived. Three weeks later he abducted Lynda Healy, another student, from her apartment. Her room-mates found bloodstains on her bed, but she was never seen again. Over the next six months, five more female college students disappeared. Several women reported being approached by a man with his arm in a plaster cast who called himself Ted. He asked them if they could help him carry some books to his car. The police now had an accurate description of Bundy and the green VW Beetle he was driving. Bundy's girlfriend started to get suspicious after finding a bag of women's clothing under his bed. She phoned the police anonymously and gave them his name, but the details of her call got buried in an avalanche of information they were receiving at the time and nothing came of it.

In October 1974 Bundy moved to Salt Lake City to study law at the University of Utah. Four female students went missing from the campus over the next month, including the seventeen-year-old daughter of the police chief. Her body was found a week later on some waste ground. She had been brutally raped, bludgeoned

# Officials Hunt Aspen Area Hills for Bundy

with a metal bar and strangled. On 8 November Bundy approached Carol DaRonch in a Salt Lake City shopping mall, telling her he was a police officer and that her car had been broken into. She accompanied him to the car park and he persuaded her to get into his car, where he attacked her. She fought him off and managed to escape. A few hours later seventeen-year-old Debby Kent was abducted from the car park of her school a few miles away. Her body has never been found.

Eight more women disappeared in Utah while Bundy was there. In January 1975, he moved to Aspen, Colorado, for a few months, and, in that time, seven women disappeared. Some of their battered bodies where found in the snow on Taylor Mountain, near a Colorado ski resort. By now bodies of young women were turning up in three different states. In Washington, police were finally making progress with their investigation. They had compiled a list of 25 suspects from the numerous reports they had received and were going through it. Bundy was on the list and was scheduled to be interviewed next when he was arrested by a highway patrol officer in Utah after failing to stop for a routine check after a spate of burglaries in the area. Forensic evidence found in the car linked him to one of the bodies in Colorado and he was extradited to Aspen to stand trial for murder. During the lengthy preliminary hearings Bundy, who was representing himself, was given permission to use the courthouse library to prepare his defence. He climbed out of a second floor window and escaped. After a week on the run a traffic cop in Aspen stopped him in a stolen car and took him back into custody.

In December 1977, while he was still being held in custody waiting for his trial to begin, Bundy escaped again, this time by cutting through the ceiling of his cell and crawling out. He escaped on New Year's Eve and was not found to be missing until the middle of the next day. By that time he was long gone and heading for Florida. He lived by shoplifting and stealing credit cards, adopting the names of the people whose cards he had stolen. On 14 January 1978 he walked into a sorority house on the campus of Florida State University in Tallahassee and mounted a frenzied attack on whoever he came across there. In less than half an hour he savagely assaulted five women,

BELOW: Portrait of 12-year-old Kimberly Leach, murdered by Ted Bundy on 9 February 1978.

killing two of them and leaving the bite mark on one that would ultimately convict him.

On 9 February he abducted twelve-year-old Kimberley Leach from the grounds of her school. He sexually assaulted her and strangled her before dumping the body in the Suwannee River Park. A few days later he tried to leave Florida in a stolen car, but was stopped yet again by traffic cops. By this time he was on the FBI's Ten Most Wanted list and was easily identified. He was sent back to Tallahassee and charged with the murders of the four women in the sorority house. At first he refused to allow an impression to be made of his teeth, no doubt realizing it could tie him to the murders. Eventually a judge ordered it to be taken by force if necessary and he had to submit.

After his conviction Bundy used every tactic in the book to delay his execution, going through appeal after appeal. He gradually gave detailed accounts of some of the attacks he had committed, hoping that, by confessing to these crimes, he would buy himself more time. At one point his attorney even asked the families of his victims to support his appeals for a stay of execution so he would have more time to reveal where the bodies that had not been recovered were hidden, but everybody who was contacted refused to help. Psychiatrists and special agents from the FBI

THEODORE ROBERT BUNDY

Bundy Left Alone in Aspen Courtroom

Leaps Out Window, Escapes Into Hills

ASPEN, Colo (AP) — Accused mur-   district court here for pretrial argu-

(Indicate page, ne
newspaper, city a

# Slay Suspect Bundy Escapes Again, Crawls Through Hole in Jail Cell

interviewed him over and over again. He told them he had returned to the bodies of some of his victims repeatedly after he had dumped them. He said he combed their hair and applied make-up to their faces before having sex with their decomposing bodies. He also said he would help the police detectives investigating the so-called Green River killings by giving them an insight into the mind of a serial killer. Detectives interviewed him, but found what he said to be of little use.

The appeals process dragged on for more than ten years. After the final appeal failed, he began to confess to killings he could not possibly have committed, having been in custody at the time of the murders. Finally, the date for his execution was set. It was going to be on 24 January 1989. A few hours before the execution Bundy gave a final TV interview to James Dobson, who belonged to an evangelical Christian organization involved in anti-pornography campaigns. It appeared a strange choice until Bundy's purpose became apparent. He blamed his crimes on the influence of pornography and tried to present himself as being as much of a victim as the women he had killed. Outside the prison thousands of people gathered and a carnival atmosphere developed. At 7.06am they cheered as the prison lights went out for a few seconds, signalling that the power in the prison had been switched to the electric chair. Two minutes later one of the most prolific serial killers in American history was dead.

OPPOSITE PAGE: Demonstrators rejoice after Ted Bundy is executed by the State of Florida on 24 January 1989.
BELOW: The body of Ted Bundy is transported to the Alachua County Medical Examiner's Office.

MURDERS
13

ATTEMPTED MURDERS
7

METHOD
BLUDGEON
HAMMER

PETER SUTCLIFFE

**Peter Sutcliffe heard voices from the heavens** instructing him to **murder prostitutes** in his home town of Leeds. When terrified prostitutes moved away in their droves – **he followed** them to Bradford to continue his killing spree – that is until a chance encounter with the police in a back alley put an **abrupt end to the Yorkshire Rippers** reign of terror.

On 5 February 1977 the body of 28-year-old Irene Richardson was found in Roundhay Park, Leeds. She had been a part-time prostitute, working in the red-light district of Chapeltown, and had been attacked the previous night. She was killed by three heavy blows to the head, with a ball-pien hammer, that shattered her skull. After she was dead, her attacker pulled some of her clothes off and stabbed her repeatedly with a sharpened screwdriver and a knife. There was no sign of a sexual element to the assault. After stabbing her, the assailant had thrown her coat over her body and driven away. Tyre tracks were found nearby, and the police identified the type of tyre, but it didn't lead them to the killer.

If there had been any doubt in their minds at this point, West Yorkshire Police now knew for certain there was a serial killer operating in the area, targeting prostitutes in Chapeltown. The parallels with the Jack the Ripper murders in Whitechapel, London, in 1888, were obvious for all to see. It didn't take long for the newspapers to come up with a name for the killer – the Yorkshire Ripper.

The first victim had been the 28-year-old mother of four Wilma McCann, a part-time prostitute who only worked when she was short of money. She was killed on 30 October 1975 by hammer blows to the head and then stabbed repeatedly. Another part-time prostitute, 42-year-old Emily Jackson, was murdered in a similar way on 20 January 1976. The police connected the two cases, but attacks on prostitutes were a common enough occurrence and the media were not all that interested. Although the police didn't realize the connection until much later, there had already been two attacks on prostitutes in Keighley and Halifax, both a short drive

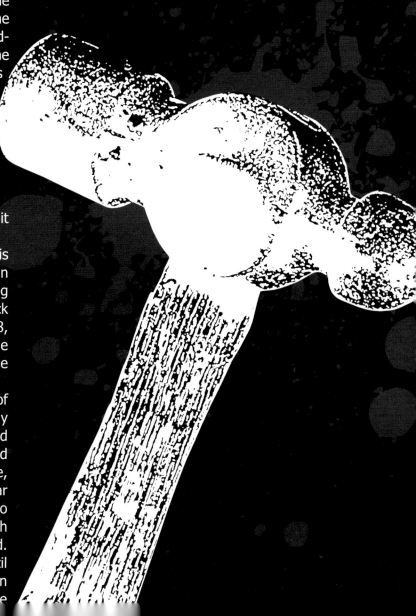

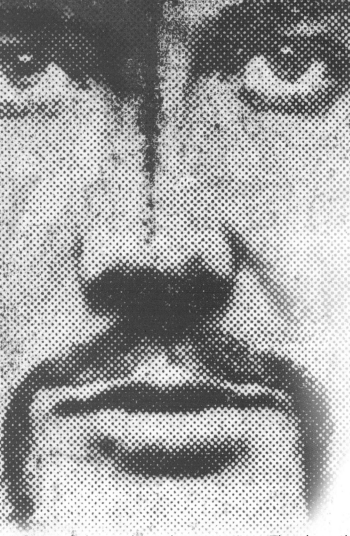

# THE MAN HAD BLACK WAVY HAIR AND A BLACK BEARD AND PICKED HER UP IN A WHITE CAR WITH RED UPHOLSTERY

from Leeds, at about the same time. They bore the same hallmarks of the murders in Leeds, except on both occasions the victims survived. It was only the first of a catalogue of mistakes and oversights the police would make which would dog the investigation throughout its course.

By the time Marcella Claxton was attacked in Roundhay Park by a man with a hammer, in May 1976, a full-scale investigation had begun. Although hit over the head several times, she survived and gave a description to the police. The man had black wavy hair and a black beard and picked her up in a white car with red upholstery. After this attack, panic spread through Chapeltown, but the media remained mostly uninterested. It was not until the murder of Irene Richardson, when the Ripper angle was introduced, that the press scented a big story. By that time many of the Chapeltown prostitutes had moved elsewhere, to London, Manchester or, if they didn't want to go that far, to Bradford.

With fewer potential victims and a greater police presence in Leeds, the Yorkshire Ripper followed the same path. On 23 April 1977 he attacked Patricia

Atkinson in her home in Bradford. She had been seen out in Bradford's red-light district that night and must have picked up the Ripper and taken him back to her flat. Once inside he struck her on the back of the head with the ball-pien hammer and carried her into the bedroom. Although she was already dead, he pulled off most of her clothes and stabbed her repeatedly in the stomach. Her body was found the next day. The Ripper had left the police another clue. There was a print from a size 7 boot on the sheets next to the body.

The next attack, on 26 June 1977, changed the public perception of the case. Jayne MacDonald was not a prostitute. She was a sixteen-year-old shop assistant walking home after a Friday night out in Leeds City Centre. She just happened to live near Chapeltown. The Ripper attacked her as she was walking along the street, hitting her over the head, stabbing her and dumping her body in a school playground. The newspapers described her as 'innocent', which she certainly was, but the implication was that murdering prostitutes was in some way not as serious as murdering other people.

With the investigation getting nowhere and the press and public demanding action, West Yorkshire Police brought in their most experienced detective, Assistant Chief Constable George Oldfield, to oversee the case. On 27 July Maureen Long survived an attack in Bradford and, on 1 October, Jean Jordan was murdered in Manchester. The Ripper left her body in a cemetery and it was ten days before it was found. In that time he had returned to the body and mutilated it further, almost cutting her head off with a piece of glass. The police found Jean Jordan's handbag nearby. There was a brand new £5 note in it and they thought the Ripper might have returned to look for it, knowing it could incriminate him. They traced the note to money paid in wages to about 8,000 people in and around Bradford. Interviews began, including one with a lorry driver called Peter Sutcliffe, who worked for a haulage company in the area. The police officers who questioned him didn't consider him to be a suspect. He was a respectable married man, who answered the questions put to him in an open and, apparently, honest manner. It is always easy to criticize in hindsight, but Sutcliffe had black wavy hair and a black beard. He was slightly built, with relatively small feet for a man, about size 7, and he owned a white car.

A woman survived an attacked in Leeds in December, but, over the next four months three more characteristic murders occurred in Bradford, Huddersfield and Manchester. The Ripper had sex with the last of these victims. It was the first time he had done so and it allowed the police to establish his blood group – type B. By this time George Oldfield was receiving letters and tapes from a man with a Sunderland accent claiming to be the Ripper. Wearside Jack, as he became called, turned out to be a hoax, but resources of manpower and money where switched to tracing him. Although not identified at the time, DNA analysis of the letters eventually led to the arrest of a Sunderland man, John Humble, in 2005. He received an eight-year prison sentence for perverting the course of justice. While the hoax was being investigated, Peter Sutcliffe was interviewed by

the police again. His car had been seen more than 30 times in the red light district of Bradford, but he didn't have a Sunderland accent and his handwriting didn't match the letters.

After an 11-month break, during which George Oldfield was removed from the investigation, the ripper struck again. On 4 April 1979, nineteen-year-old office worker Josephine Whittaker was murdered. Then Barbara Leach, a student from Bradford, was killed in September. Another break of almost a year occurred, until 18 August 1980. Marguerite Walls was hit over the head with a hammer as she was walking home after working late in Leeds. Two more attacks followed in October and November. Both women were seriously injured but survived. Jacqueline Hill, a twenty-year-old Leeds University student, didn't survive the attack on her on 7 November.

On 2 January 1981 two police officers on a routine patrol saw a car parked on a quiet backstreet of Sheffield. It was known as a place were prostitutes took their clients, so they decided to investigate. The driver of the car gave his name as Peter Williams and said the woman with him was his girlfriend, although he couldn't remember her name. One of the officers recognized her – she was Olive Curry, a known prostitute. They asked the man to step out of the car while they phoned the station to check the licence plates. He asked if he could relieve himself and went behind an oil storage tank nearby. The licence plates didn't match the car. The man told them his real name, Peter Sutcliffe. He said he had lied because he didn't want his wife to find out he had picked up a prostitute. He also admitted stealing the licence plates from a car near Dewsbury, a few miles south of Leeds. The officers arrested him and took him to the local police station in Sheffield. Again he asked to go to the toilet and was allowed to go unaccompanied. As he had been caught with a prostitute, the Sheffield Police rang the Ripper Squad, as the investigation was informally called, to report it to them. It was the established routine for any arrest involving prostitutes, whatever the circumstances.

The next morning Sutcliffe was transferred to Dewsbury Police Station to be interviewed about the stolen licence plates. A detective from the Ripper Squad drove the few miles from Leeds to speak to him as well. A blood test showed Sutcliffe was type B and he matched the descriptions. One of the arresting officers, on being told Sutcliffe was being interviewed by the Ripper Squad, returned to the scene of the arrest to look behind the oil tank. He found a hammer and a sharpened screwdriver. Shortly afterwards a knife was found in the cistern of a toilet in the police station.

By the next morning, Sutcliffe's house in Bradford had been searched and more hammers and screwdrivers had been found. More detectives from the Ripper Squad arrived in Dewsbury. On being told he was in serious trouble, Sutcliffe asked them if they wanted to talk to him about the Yorkshire Ripper. A full confession soon followed. It took 17 hours to record all the details. After more than five years, the police finally had their man.

The trial was held at the Old Bailey in London in May 1981. Sutcliffe pleaded guilty to manslaughter on the grounds of diminished responsibility, saying he had heard the voice of God directing him to kill women. The judge rejected the plea and a jury found him guilty of

13 murders and 7 attempted murders. He was sentenced to life imprisonment with a recommendation he serve at least 30 years. Soon after being sent to prison, he was transferred to Broadmoor, a high-security psychiatric hospital.

After the trial an enquiry was held into the Ripper investigation, parts of which were made public in 2006. It emerged that Peter Sutcliffe had been interviewed 11 times during the five-year period between the first attack and his capture. He first attacked a woman in 1969, and the author of the report was certain Sutcliffe had attacked many other women as well as the 20 attacks he was charged with. Although there has been speculation that Sutcliffe did not act alone, the section of the report dealing with 'known associates' has not been released.

OPPOSITE PAGE: Six of the young women murdered by Peter Sutcliffe, known as the Yorkshire Ripper. BELOW: Police hold back crowds outside Dewsbury court, Yorkshire as Peter Sutcliffe appears after his arrest in connnection with the 'Yorkshire Ripper' murders.

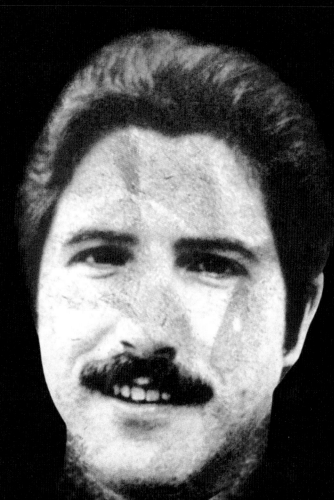

**MURDERS 10**

**METHOD TORTURE STRANGLE**

**A.K.A. HILLSIDE STRANGLERS**

**KEN BIANCHI & ANGELO BUONO**

**The Hillside Stranglers were a deadly duo united in blood-lust. Together they raped and murdered scores of dispossessed local girls, before dumping their bodies in scrub land on the hills above Los Angeles. Police were on the trail of Ken Bianchi and Angelo Buono, but before the end each man would attempt to betray the other in order to save his own skin.**

Ken Bianchi was adopted by Nicholas and Frances Bianchi when he was three months old. His biological mother was a prostitute in Rochester, New York, and had given him up for adoption at birth. He grew into a bright and good-looking boy, but had a short attention span and was prone to temper tantrums. By his teens he was getting into trouble for a string of petty crimes and was failing at school. He got married at eighteen, but it didn't last. After that he was only interested in short-term casual relationships. About the only thing he wanted to do was join the police force, but he didn't have good enough grades and ended up working as a security guard. In late 1975 he decided to make a change in his life and moved to Glendale, on the outskirts of Los Angeles. Until he could afford a place of his own, he stayed with his adoptive cousin, Angelo Buono, who he soon began to look up to as a sort of elder brother.

Buono was not much of a role model. He was 17 years older than Bianchi and had something of a reputation. He had been married four times and had eight children. All four wives had left him because he was violent and sexually abusive. He even bragged he had 'broken-in' one of his stepdaughters when she was fourteen. Then there was his criminal record – for rape, assault and stealing cars. Despite this, there were always girls hanging around him, however badly he treated them. If he needed the money, he was not above pimping them out either.

Bianchi applied to join the Glendale Police Department and was rejected. After moving into his own place, he had the rent and the repayments on his

# THEY KEPT THE TWO GIRLS AS VIRTUAL PRISONERS, THREATENING THEM WITH EXTREME VIOLENCE UNLESS THEY DID AS THEY WERE TOLD

car to pay. So to earn some money Buono suggested going into business together, pimping out two young runaways who were hanging around. They kept the two girls as virtual prisoners, threatening them with extreme violence unless they did as they were told. With the help of a lawyer one of them knew, both managed to escape. Buono and Bianchi needed replacements. They went out looking, carrying fake police IDs with them, so they could 'arrest' any likely looking suspects.

Between October 1977 and February 1978 naked bodies of girls and young women were found dumped on waste ground in northern Los Angeles or in the hills above Glendale. All had ligature marks on their ankles, wrists and around their necks. They had been tied up, viciously sexually assaulted and, with increasing savagery as time went on, tortured, then strangled to death. The first victim was Yolanda Washington, a nineteen-year-old prostitute, well known to the Los Angeles Police Department. Her body was found in a cemetery in north Los Angeles, not far from the Warner Brothers Studio. At the time the LAPD didn't pay much attention. Murder was an everyday event in Los Angeles and the cops regarded it as an occupational hazard for prostitutes.

The second victim was sixteen-year-old Judy Miller, a destitute runaway.

Her body was found in Glendale on 31 October. It hardly raised an eyebrow with the LAPD either, although they did notice the similarity with the previous killing and that Judy Miller had been killed somewhere else and the body dumped where it was found. An autopsy showed she had been raped by two men. A week later the body of Lissa Kastin, a 21-year-old waitress, was found near Glendale Country Club. She was last seen leaving work the night before. The ligature marks on her body were the same and she had been sexually assaulted. The police were beginning to take notice. It looked like there were a pair of serial killers working together in the Glendale area. The police thought the killers had probably known their victims.

Two schoolgirls, Dolores Cepeda, 12, and Sonja Johnston, 14, went missing on 13 November after getting off a school bus to walk the rest of the way home. A week later both bodies were found on a hillside near the Dodger Stadium in Charvez Ravine. On the same day another body was found in the hills near Glendale. It was twenty-year-old student Kristina Weckler. All three were victims of the same two men. The Los Angeles newspapers were interested now and came up with the name 'the Hillside Strangler'. The police hadn't told them two men were involved.

RIGHT: Kenneth Bianchi arrives at court, charged with the murders of five women in the Los Angeles area in late 1977 and early 1978.
BELOW: Angelo Buono talks to a young woman outside his upholstery shop, as a press conference is held naming him as a suspect in the Hillside Stranglers case.

Over the next few weeks three more bodies were found around Glendale and north Los Angeles. A task force was set up containing officers from the LAPD, the Los Angeles Sheriff's Office and the Glendale Police Department, as bodies had been found in all three jurisdictions. Despite a history of antagonism between them, for once all three law enforcement agencies managed to cooperate with each other. Even so the investigation didn't seem to be getting anywhere – there was not much to go on. A witness had seen two men bundle one of the victims into a car and had described a man of about 40 with a Latin appearance and a younger man. The next day she had been phoned by a man with a New York accent telling her she would be killed if she talked to the police.

On 13 December 1977 Kimberley Martin's body was found on a construction site in Los Angeles. She had been a prostitute who worked for a modelling agency, as it was called. A man phoned the agency and asked for a girl to come to an apartment, which was empty when the police checked it out. The call came from a pay phone in the Hollywood Public Library. They were the best leads the police had, but neither amounted to anything. After that nothing happened for three months. On 13 February 1978 a car was found in a ravine in Angeles Crest, north of the city. The body of the owner, twenty-year-old Cindy Hudspeth, was in the trunk. Her body showed all the signs that she was the tenth victim of the Hillside Stranglers. She had lived in Glendale, in the same street as one of the other victims, and the police were certain that at least one of the killers was from the same area, but they still didn't have much to go on. It was the last of the characteristic murders in the Los Angeles and Glendale area. Whoever they were, it looked like the Hillside Stranglers had stopped.

Almost a year later, in January 1979, two students from Western Washington University in Bellingham, Washington State, went missing. Karen Mandic and

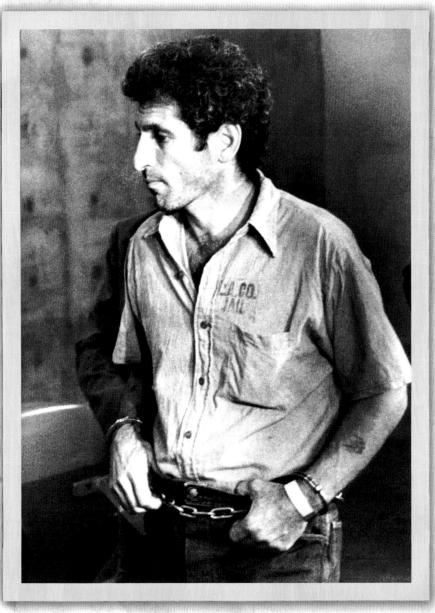

Diane Wilder were 22-year-old room-mates and it was unlike them to go away without letting anyone know. It emerged that one of them had been asked to house sit an empty property by a man she knew who worked for a security company. He was called Ken Bianchi and had moved to Bellingham from the Los Angeles area in the past year with his girlfriend, and their young son. The police went to Bianchi's house to ask him if he knew what had happened to the two missing women. He said he didn't know anything about it and had been at a meeting of the Sheriff's Reserves that night.

Two days later a car abandoned in woodland outside town was reported to the police. The bodies of the two girls were found in it. Both had been raped and strangled. The police went to see Bianchi again and searched his home. They didn't find anything there to connect him to the murders, but they did find property he had stolen from the security jobs he had worked. He was arrested and held in custody while a thorough forensic investigation was carried out. Samples of his hair were recovered from the empty house and the car and strands of the carpet from the house were on one of the girl's clothes. The Washington

# UNDER HYPNOSIS HE HAD SAID THAT HIS OTHER SELF, WHICH HE CALLED STEVE WALKER, HAD RAPED, TORTURED AND KILLED ALL THOSE WOMEN

police phoned the LAPD. Bianchi had lived in the same building as one of the victims of the Hillside Stranglers. Two more had been seen in the vicinity shortly before they disappeared. The evidence against Bianchi was coming together. An LAPD officer travelled up to Bellingham and found that jewellery recovered from Bianchi's house matched items owned by two more of the Hillside Stranglers' victims. It looked like they had got one of them. The question was, could they get the other one?

It was not hard to connect Angelo Buono with Ken Bianchi, but there was no hard evidence to connect Buono to the murders. The police offered Bianchi a deal. If he gave up Buono he wouldn't face the death sentence and could serve his time in California rather than in the infamous Walla Walla Prison in Washington. Bianchi confessed, but claimed insanity. At his trail for the murder of the two students, his defence rested on a diagnosis by a psychiatrist that he was suffering from multiple personality disorder. Under hypnosis he had said that his other self, which he called Steve Walker, had raped, tortured and killed all those women. The psychiatrist might have believed him, but the prosecution didn't. They produced evidence showing that Steve Walker was an alias Bianchi had used to set himself up as a bogus psychiatrist in Los Angeles. Books about psychiatry and hypnosis were found in his house. It was obvious to the jury he was faking it. They found him guilty.

In the meantime Buono had been arrested in Glendale. Forensic evidence against him had been found, but the case hinged on Bianchi's testimony. He was not the most convincing witness in the world and, at the start of the trial, the prosecutor from the district attorney's office lost his nerve and moved to have the case against Buono dismissed. In a highly unusual move, the judge refused the motion and transferred the prosecution to the Attorney General of California. The trial dragged on for two years. At one point Bianchi appeared to be backing out of the deal he had made in Washington, until he was gently reminded of the conditions in Walla Walla. Eventually, in October 1983, Buono was found guilty on nine counts of murder, but not guilty of the murder of Yolanda Washington. He was spared the death sentence and was sentenced to life without the possibility of parole. Initially he was sent to Folsom State Prison and then transferred to Calipatria, where he died of a heart attack in 2002. Despite being promised he would serve his time in California, Bianchi was returned to Washington and is serving life in Walla Walla.

ABOVE: Kenneth Bianchi sobs in court on 19 October 1979.

OPPOSITE PAGE: Angelo Buono arrives at court on 22 October 1979, charged with the murders of ten women.

MURDERS
15

METHOD
STRANGLE
DROWN

SENTENCE
LIFE
IMPRISONMENT

DENNIS
NILSEN

# Dennis Nilsen was so lonely that he murdered his lovers to keep them nearby, sometimes cuddling up to a cadaver as he watched TV, or laying it next to him as he slept. It wasn't until his neighbours complained of problems with the drains, that his murderous secret was uncovered.

It was already dark on 8 February 1983 by the time Michael Cattran from Dyno-Rod, the drain clearing company, got to 23 Cranley Gardens in Muswell Hill, North London. It was a large house in a tree-lined street, which had been converted into six flats. Five of the residents had been complaining to the landlord about blocked drains for several days, although the man who lived in the attic flat said he was not having a problem. In Cattran's line of business, dealing with foul smells went with the job, but even he must have recoiled when he lifted the manhole cover over the sewage outlet. The inspection pit was about a foot deep in rotting flesh. He told the residents he would come back in the morning when he could see what he was doing. When Cattran lifted the manhole cover again the next day, almost all the rotting flesh had gone. There were just a few bones and a piece of flesh stuck in the outflow pipe. One of the residents told him she had heard the man from the attic flat going

up and down the stairs repeatedly during the night. Cattran phoned the police and it didn't take them long to establish the flesh and bones were human remains.

Dennis Nilsen, who lived in the attic flat, had gone to work as usual that morning. By the time he returned to his flat in the evening, there were three policemen waiting for him. They told him they wanted to talk to him about the drains and he expressed surprise, wondering why they would be interested in such a thing. One of them asked him where the rest of the body was. He calmly told them it was in two plastic bags in his wardrobe. They arrested Nilsen and he said he would explain everything at the police station. Once there he confessed to 15 or 16 murders, he couldn't remember exactly how many.

Dennis Nilsen was born in 1945 in Fraserburgh, a fishing town on the north-east coast of Scotland. His father was Norwegian and had come to Scotland during World War II to escape

# THE INSPECTION PIT WAS ABOUT A FOOT DEEP IN ROTTING FLESH

the Nazi invasion of Norway and had married Nilsen's mother, a local Scottish girl. After years of fighting, Nilsen's parents divorced when he was four years old. His mother remarried and he was sent to live with his grandparents, who were very strictly religious. He would say after his arrest that seeing the body of his grandfather, who died when Nilsen was seven, had a profound psychological effect on him and he became fascinated by death. Nilsen joined the army when he was sixteen, serving for 11 years as a cook and learning the butchery skills he would later use to dispose of the bodies of his victims. During his time in the army he also had his first homosexual experiences. After leaving the army, he joined the police force, but quickly realized it was not for him and resigned within a year. He got a job with the Civil Service, working in a job centre in central London, where he would meet unemployed boys and, occasionally, take them out for a meal and a drink after he finished work.

In 1978 Nilsen was living in a garden flat in Cricklewood, north-west London. That year he spent a lonely Christmas on his own. On 30 December, he picked up a boy in a pub and took him back to the flat. After they had had sex, Nilsen thought the boy would leave and he would be left on his own again. To stop this happening, Nilsen waited until the boy was asleep and strangled him with a tie. To make sure he was dead, Nilsen held the boy's head in a bucket of water for several minutes. He then washed the body and hid it under the floorboards in his flat. A week later, he pulled the body out and washed it again. Finally, in August 1979, he dismembered the body, wrapped it in an old carpet and burnt it on a bonfire in the garden, throwing an old tyre on the fire to cover the smell of burning flesh. The boy was not positively identified until 2006. He was fourteen-year-old Stephen Holmes, who had been reported missing a few days before Nilsen killed him.

Shortly after disposing of Stephen Holmes's body, Nilsen invited Andrew Ho, a student from Hong Kong, back to Cricklewood. Nilsen attempted to strangle him

while they were having sex, but Ho fought him off and escaped. Despite initially reporting the attack to the police, Ho decided not to continue with the prosecution and charges against Nilsen were dropped. In December 1979, Kenneth Ockenden, was not so lucky. The nineteen-year-old Canadian student met Nilsen in a bar and, despite having a ticket to fly back to Canada the following day, agreed to go back to Nilsen's flat for the night. The pattern Nilsen had established with Stephen Holmes repeated itself. He strangled the young Canadian and hid his body under the floorboards. On several occasions he retrieved the body and propped it up next to him as he watched TV in the evening and then slept with it in the bed next to him at night.

By May 1980, Nilsen had disposed of Ockenden's body in the garden and replaced him under the floorboards with the body of Martin Duffey, a sixteen-year-old homeless boy. A few days later Billy Sutherland, 21, a male prostitute from Scotland, joined Duffey. Nilsen had strangled Sutherland with his bare hands. Over the next 14 months there would be seven more victims. Nilsen claims he either didn't know their names or could not remember who they were. He has only given vague descriptions of them and all seven remain unidentified.

During this period Douglas Stewart, a barman in the Golden Lion pub in Soho, had a lucky escape. In November 1980 he accepted Nilsen's invitation to go back to his flat. During the night, Nilsen attempted to strangle Stewart, but he woke up and pushed Nilsen away. Stewart reported the attempted murder to the police, but they treated it as a domestic squabble between two homosexual men and took no action against Nilsen.

ABOVE: Dennis Nilsen being transported to Highgate Court, North London charged with the murder of 20-year-old Stephen Sinclair.

The last known victim in Cricklewood was the 24-year-old homeless man Malcolm Barlow. On 18 September Nilsen came across the young man slumped in a doorway, took him back to his flat and called an ambulance. The following day Barlow returned to the flat to thank Nilsen for helping him. Nilsen invited Barlow in and strangled him during the night. Not long after this, Nilsen's landlord informed him that he had to move out of the flat and offered him alternative accommodation in Muswell Hill. By this time Nilsen had accumulated a number of bodies in the flat. Before moving out he cut them up and burned them on another bonfire. He collected their internal organs in a bag and left them outside by the garden fence for rats, urban foxes and other scavengers to find.

Although there were no floorboards in the flat in Muswell Hill and Nilsen didn't have access to the garden, by this time he was too out of control to stop killing. In November 1981 he picked up Paul Nobbs in the Golden Lion in Soho. In the morning Nobbs woke up in Nilsen's bed to find red marks around his neck. He went to his doctor, who told him it looked like someone had tried to strangle him, but Nobb's decided not to report it to the police. Not long after this, Nilsen attempted to strangle Carl Stotter while he was sleeping in Nilsen's flat. Stotter, well known in the gay community as the drag queen Khara Le Fox, woke up while Nilsen was attempting to drown him in the bath and fought him off. Stotter didn't approach the police either until after Nilsen was arrested. The obvious lack of trust between London's gay community and the police undoubtedly contributed to the number of murders Nilsen committed before he was caught.

After two failures, Nilsen's next victim was John Howlett, another well-known figure in Soho, where he was known as John the Guardsman. After drinking together in a bar, Howlett accepted Nilsen's invitation to accompany him back to the flat in Muswell Hill. There was a disagreement between them and Nilsen asked Howlett to leave, but he refused. Nilsen attacked Howlett, attempting to strangle him, but he fought back. The struggle lasted several minutes before Nilsen overcame Howlett, finally drowning him in the bath after he was unconscious. With nowhere in the flat to hide the body, Nilsen decided to cut it up and flush it down the toilet. He boiled some of the body parts, including the head, in a pan on the cooker to make

BELOW: A coffin is removed from the 'house of horrors' in Cranley Gardens, Muswell Hill, London.

# THE CHOPPING BLOCK HE USED TO DISMEMBER HIS VICTIMS AND THE COOKING POT HE HAD BOILED THEM IN WERE SHOWN TO THE COURT

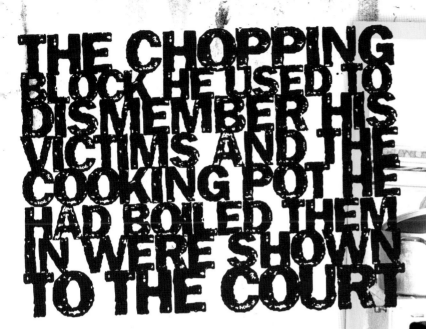

it easier to remove the flesh and stored the larger bones in a tea chest.

Nilsen claimed not to remember much about his next victim. He was a homeless heroin addict called Graham Allen. According to Nilsen, the only part he could remember was making Allen an omelette and then him being unconscious in the bath. Nilsen left the body there for three days before disposing of it in the same way as he had the previous one. His final victim was Stephen Sinclair, who was addicted to heroin. It was Nilsen's attempts to flush this body away that would lead to his exposure and arrest. As well as the remains found in the drain, police recovered the parts of the body still in Nilsen's flat, including the partially boiled head.

Nilsen was charged with the murder of the six people who could be identified together with two counts of attempted murder. At his trial in October 1983, Nilsen entered a plea of diminished responsibility. As the evidence against him was overwhelming, the defence rested on the jury accepting this plea. The chopping block he used to dismember his victims and the cooking pot he had boiled them in were shown to the court and the detailed confession he had written after his arrest was read

out in full. Witnesses for the prosecution included Douglas Stewart, Paul Nobbs and Carl Stotter. Nilsen attempted to discredit their testimony by exposing some details they had got wrong, but, in doing so, succeeded in showing himself to be cold and calculating. After considerable deliberation, the jury came to a majority decision of 10 to 2 in favour of Nilsen being guilty on all counts. He was sentenced to life imprisonment with a recommendation he serve a minimum of 25 years. This minimum term expires in 2008, at which point Nilsen will be eligible for parole.

ABOVE: Anne Davies views the pot on the stove used by Dennis Nilsen to boil the severed heads of his victims, at an exhibition staged by Scotland Yard's Forensic Science Laboratory in South London to celebrate 50 years of analyzing crime.

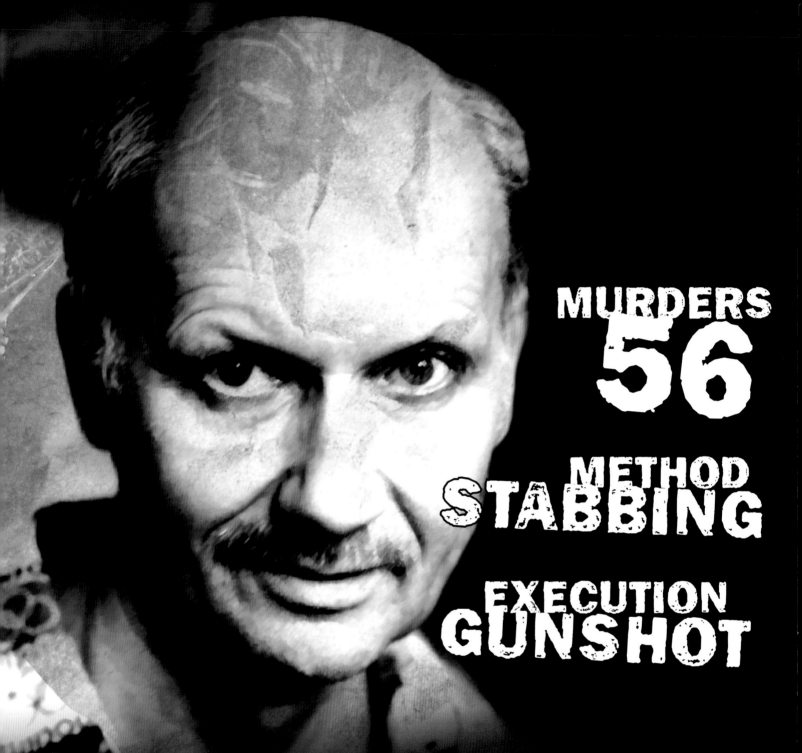

MURDERS
**56**

METHOD
STABBING

EXECUTION
GUNSHOT

ANDREI
CHIKATILO

The communist regime in Russia believed that vicious serial killings were a decadent Western phenomenon. Consequently Andrei Chikatilo was allowed to kill again and again and, as a party member, the soviet authorities turned a blind-eye to his depraved crimes.

In the 1980s the police investigating the mounting number of murders occurring in the Rostov area of the Soviet Union knew they were looking for a prolific serial killer. The Soviet authorities refused to admit the possibility. According to communist doctrine, serial killers were a symptom of the corruption and decadence of Western capitalist countries, particularly the USA. Consequently, it couldn't happen in the Soviet Union. This was a serious obstacle for the investigation to overcome. The strictly-controlled Soviet media couldn't report any details of the murders indicating a serial killer was involved. It meant they didn't give out descriptions of the man the police were looking for. They couldn't even warn the public of the danger, because in doing so they would be admitting that there was only one killer.

Almost all the rapes and murders were happening in the vicinity of the public transport system. Bodies were found in strips of woodland near bus and train stations. The police were sure the man was approaching passengers in the stations or on board buses and trains and luring them into the woodland, but they were not allowed to tell people to look out for a man behaving suspiciously in these locations.

The inflexibility of the Soviet system certainly contributed to the length of time it took the police to catch Andrei Chikatilo, but the police themselves have to share some of the blame. They could have stopped him after he had killed for the first time. In 1978 Chikatilo was working as a teacher in Shakhty, a city about 80 km (50 miles) north of Rostov. He was married and had two children, despite being almost impotent. He only became sexually aroused when he was with children and had already left one teaching job after complaints were made against him. He bought a shed by the river near Shakhty and lured a nine-year-old girl into it by promising to give her some sweets. Once inside the shed, he tried to rape her. She struggled and he stabbed her repeatedly in the stomach. As he killed her, he became aroused and ejaculated. The girl was reported missing and one of her friends told police she had seen her with a tall thin man. An artist's impression was drawn up and shown around Shakhty. It resembled Chikatilo, and the principal of the school where he worked gave his name to the police. They searched the shed and found bloodstains. He was arrested, but, after his wife provided him with an alibi, he was released. The police then beat a confession

out of another man, who was tried for the murder, found guilty and executed. Had they investigated this murder properly, the lives of at least 55 people might have been saved.

After coming so close to being caught, Chikatilo didn't kill again for more than three years. In 1981 he lost his teaching job after more complaints of inappropriate behaviour with children. He was a member of the Communist Party, so the complaints against him were not taken any further and he was given a job as a clerk in a factory in Shakhty. The job involved travelling around the Rostov area, with occasional business trips to other parts of the Soviet Union. Over the next two years he killed 14 people. At first his victims were all young women. He lured them into woodland with the promise of money and alcohol and, once there, attacked them. Most were

# AS HE KILLED HER, HE BECAME AROUSED AND EJACULATED

ABOVE: The polluted Kizitirinka river which runs through Aviator's park where the bodies of two of Andrei Chikatilo's victims were found.

stabbed repeatedly in the stomach and had their eyes gauged out. They were then disembowelled and some internal organs and their genitals were removed. It was not long before Chikatilo began to attack children of both sexes as well as young women. It was probably easier to lure them into the woods, but he killed them in the same way. As time went on, the attacks became more and more frenzied. He bit out the tongues of some of his victims and castrated some of the boys.

As more bodies were found, one of the leading detectives in the Soviet Union, Major Mikhail Fetisov, was sent to Rostov from Moscow to lead the investigation. Known sex offenders and men recently released from mental institutions were interrogated, and confessions were extracted from a number of them. As some of the victims were boys, known homosexuals were also targeted. The only result of these tactics was to divert resources away from catching the real killer. While the men who had confessed were being held in custody, the killings continued.

In 1984 there were 15 characteristic murders. A forensic expert assigned to the case gathered samples of semen from some of the crime scenes. Once analysed, it suggested the killer had blood type AB. By this time, the investigation had recognized the connection between the location of the killings and the public transport system. Patrols were mounted at bus and train stations. A plain-clothes police officer watching Rostov Bus Station in September 1984 noticed a middle-aged man approaching young women, trying to engage them in conversation. The man didn't succeed with any of the women and the police officer watched while he picked up a prostitute and engaged in a public sex act with her.

He arrested the man. It was Andrei Chikatilo. On being questioned about his behaviour in the bus station he explained he was on a business trip and missed the company of women. A blood test showed his blood type was not AB and he was ruled out as a suspect for the rapes and murders. It was only realized several years later that the blood type established by testing a man's semen does not always match the actual blood type of that person. Chikatilo admitted the offence with the prostitute and was given a one-year prison sentence, although, as he was a party member, he only served three months.

With the investigation apparently going nowhere, Fetisov was replaced by another leading detective from Moscow, Inspector Issa Kostoyev. After another close encounter with the police, Chikatilo became aware of the investigation. For 18 months he stopped killing in the Rostov area, but, as would later become apparent when the police checked details of his business trips, he was responsible for a number of murders around Moscow and other parts of the Soviet Union. By the middle of 1987 he couldn't wait for business trips to come around and started to kill nearer to home again. In 1988 a wave of killings occurred. Eight bodies of

women and children were found, mostly near the main railway line leading out of Rostov. Only one person is known to have been killed in 1989, but there were nine victims in 1990.

The police were becoming increasingly desperate for results by this time. They decided on a risky plan. Uniformed police officers were stationed in all but three of the railway stations along the main line out of Rostov, with instructions to make themselves as visible as possible. The idea was to try to tempt the killer into attacking someone at one of the three stations where there appeared to be no police presence. Plain-clothes officers were watching these stations and the surrounding areas, and there were female police officers on the platforms to act as lures to the killer. The obvious danger of this plan was it required the murderer to strike again before he could be caught. On 6 November 1990 a young women was raped and murdered near one of the three stations. Chikatilo was stopped nearby and questioned, but the body of his victim had not been found at that point and he was allowed to go. Afterwards, checks were carried out on all the people spoken to by the officers at the station. Chikatilo's name had cropped up a number of times

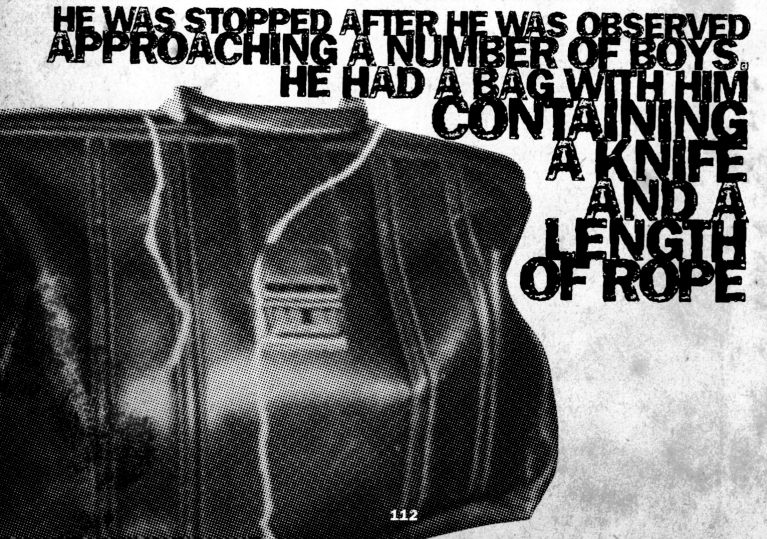

**HE WAS STOPPED AFTER HE WAS OBSERVED APPROACHING A NUMBER OF BOYS. HE HAD A BAG WITH HIM CONTAINING A KNIFE AND A LENGTH OF ROPE**

before in the investigation. He was put under surveillance and on 20 November he was stopped after he was observed approaching a number of boys. He had a bag with him containing a knife and a length of rope, which provided the police with enough grounds to arrest him.

Inspector Kostoyev was convinced he had the right man and led the interrogation himself. After getting nowhere over a period of ten days, he changed tack and brought a psychiatrist in to talk to Chikatilo. Rather than adopt the aggressive approach of the police officers, the psychiatrist talked to Chikatilo about his childhood during the Nazi invasion of the Ukraine and the sexual problems he had experienced throughout his life. Chikatilo began to open up to the psychiatrist and eventually said he was ready to confess. He was presented with a formal statement compiled by the police. It accused him of the murder of 36 people. After reading it, he admitted his guilt and confessed to 20 more killings not included in the statement, going back to the murder of the nine-year-old girl in 1978. After confessing, he explained the motivation behind the murders, telling the police he could only get sexually aroused while he was in the process of killing people. He stabbed the victim's eyes because he believed in the superstition that the image of the last thing people saw remained in their eyes after death.

Although Chikatilo confessed to 56 murders, three of the bodies were never found, so he was charged with 53 counts of murder. During the trial, beginning on 14 April 1992, he was held in an iron cage constructed in the middle of the courtroom. It was supposed to protect him from the relatives of victims who attended the trial, but it also made him look like a wild beast. Chikatilo spent most of the trial acting as if he was not interested in the proceedings. Occasionally he launched into a rant against the judge and, on two occasions,

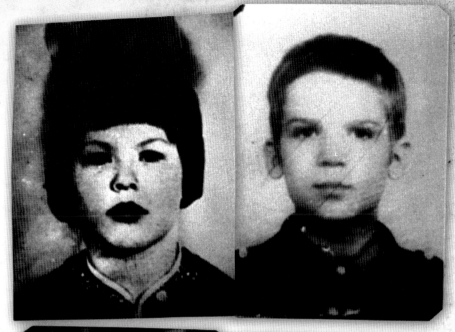

pulled his trousers down, exposing himself to the court. The defence attempted to introduce psychiatric reports to demonstrate Chikatilo was insane, but the judge would not allow it. After the trial was over, the judge took two months to reach a verdict. On 14 October he pronounced Chikatilo guilty on all but one of the 53 charges of murder and sentenced him to death. The sentence was carried out on 14 February 1994. Chikatilo was led from his cell in Rostov Prison to a soundproof room, where he was executed by a single gunshot to the back of his head.

ABOVE: Portraits of one girl and three young boys murdered by Andrei Chikatilo.

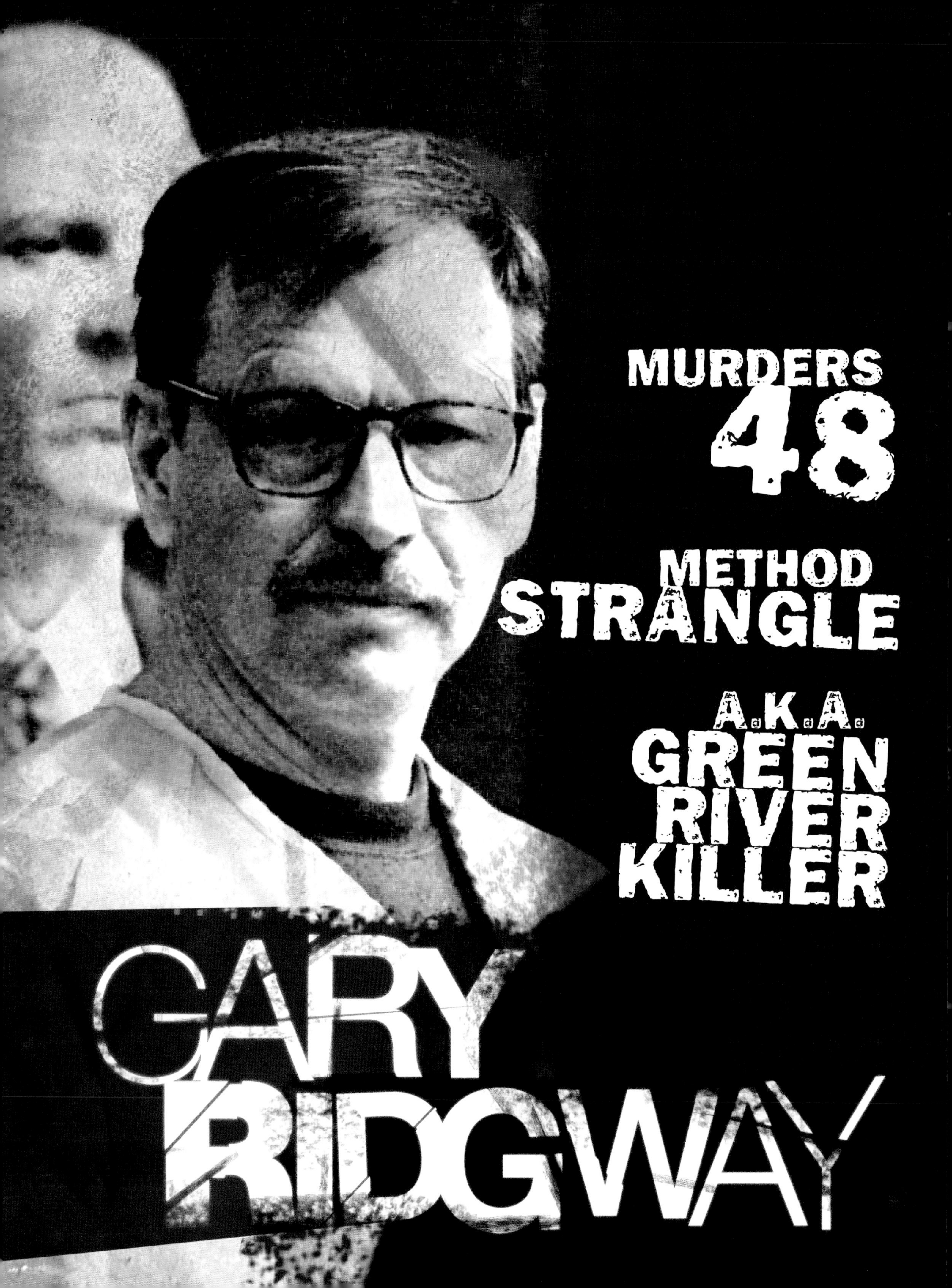

MURDERS
**48**

METHOD
**STRANGLE**

A.K.A.
**GREEN
RIVER
KILLER**

**GARY
RIDGWAY**

**Gary Ridgway attacked local prostitutes and dumped their bodies in close vicinity of the Green River, Washington State. Police regarded murder as an occupational hazard for prostitutes, and so weren't quick to assign resources to his capture. But as the bodies began to mount up they realized they had better start looking for the Green River Killer.**

The Green River flows down from the Cascade Mountains in Washington State, becoming known as the Duwamish River as it enters the city of Seattle and, where it runs out into Elliott Sound, the Duwamish Waterway. In August 1982, a fisherman in a boat on the river just outside the Seattle city limits found the body of a young woman floating beneath the surface of the water. Within seconds he saw another body. He called the police, who retrieved the two bodies from the river and, in a subsequent search of the area, found a third body not far from the riverbank. All three were young women who had been strangled to death. The body on the bank proved to be Opal Mills, sixteen, who had been

killed within the past 24 hours. The other two were Marcia Chapman, 31 who had been dead for a little over a week, and Cynthia Hinds, seventeen She had been strangled within the las few days.

In the six months previous to this discovery, three other bodies of young women had also been found either in the river or in close proximity to it. Al three had also been strangled, but the deaths had not been linked. Now the body count had reached six and it was obvious their deaths were connected. A task force of detectives was formed in King County, the district where all the bodies were found. They established straight away that all the victims had been prostitutes who worked along the main strip in Seattle, where the majority of clients picked up prostitutes in thei vehicles. It became apparent that a serial killer was picking up prostitutes and taking them to an unknown location. Once there he strangled them and then dumped the bodies either in the Green River or close to it.

Having established that much, the investigation didn't get much further. The prostitutes of Seattle didn't trust the police any more than prostitutes do anywhere else and gave them very little information about the women who had gone missing. Appeals to the general public had the opposite effect. The police were swamped with much more information than they could deal with, but almost all of it was of little or no use. The Green River Killer, as the strangler became known, was only just getting started. Between September 1982 and April 1983, 14 more prostitutes, all aged between 16 and 23, were reported missing in Seattle. Bodies were beginning to turn up in rubbish dumps and on waste ground around the city and the surrounding area. The task force identified various suspects, including a butcher who had raped two prostitutes in 1982 and a taxi driver who knew five of the missing women, but none of them was the Green River Killer.

On 30 April 1983 a nineteen-year-old prostitute called Marie Malvar was reported missing by her boyfriend. He had seen her getting into a dark coloured pick-up truck driven by a man and, when she didn't return, contacted the police. A few days later he saw the same truck in Seattle again and followed it back to a house. He rang the police again and they spoke to Gary Ridgway, the owner of the truck. He was recently divorced from his second wife, with whom he had a son, and worked as a painter for the Kenworth Truck Company in Renton, just outside Seattle. To get to work from his house he had to drive along the main strip every day. The police asked him if he knew Marie Malvar and he denied all knowledge of her. They were satisfied with his answers and didn't consider him to be a suspect. Had they pursued the investigation further, they might have reached a very different conclusion.

During the summer and autumn of 1983 another nine prostitutes went missing in Seattle. Bodies were being found near Sea-Tac Airport and Salt Lake, dumped on waste ground and partially covered with rubbish and vegetation. By the end of 1983 there were 18 confirmed victims of the Green River Killer, but there were others that the police had unaccountably left off the list. There was also a growing list of prostitutes who had been reported missing. It appeared to the people of Seattle that the police didn't know what

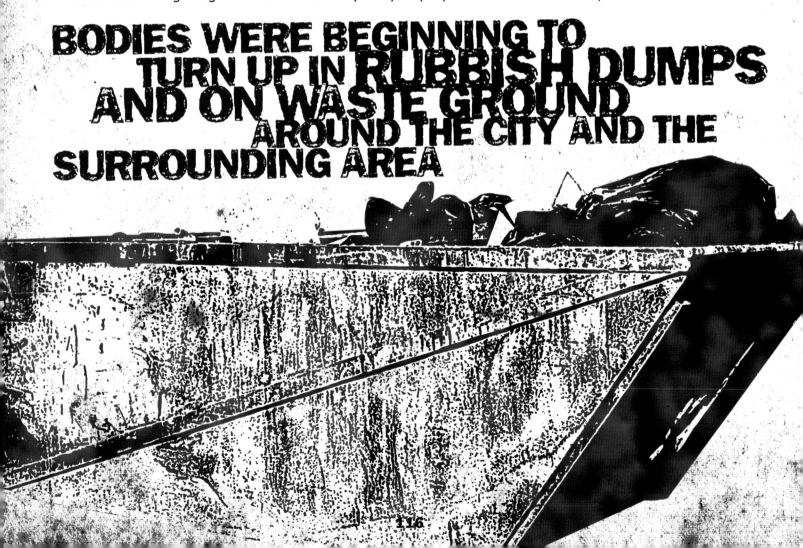

## BODIES WERE BEGINNING TO TURN UP IN RUBBISH DUMPS AND ON WASTE GROUND AROUND THE CITY AND THE SURROUNDING AREA

they were doing and were getting nowhere. They had the most prolific serial killer in American history on their hands and they didn't have a clue who he was.

The following year bodies began to turn up in a wider variety of places, some as much as 65 km (40 miles) out of Seattle, and the killer was now partially burying them in the ground. Two bodies were found in Oregon. It looked as if the killer had taken them there in an attempt to confuse the police even further. Then, towards the end of 1984, reports of prostitutes going missing began to dry up. Bodies were still being discovered, but less frequently than before and most of those that were found had been killed several months earlier. The official count had now reached 28, but everyone involved with the case knew, that in reality, there were well over 40 victims. By this time the investigation was flagging badly. The total lack of success had demoralized the detectives on the task force to such an extent that no discernible progress was being made at all. Over the next three years the investigation was gradually wound down, even though the discovery of a steady stream of bodies were still being reported.

A renewed burst of energy in the investigation occurred in 1987. It focused on one particular suspect – Gary Ridgway. Detectives digging into his past found he had been arrested in 1980 near Sea-Tac airport after he attempted to choke a prostitute while they were in his truck. At the time he said it was self-defence, as she had attacked him first, and he was let off. Then, in 1982, he had been stopped by the police with Keli McGinness, a known prostitute, and was let off again with a warning. McGinness was murdered by the Green River Killer in 1983, the same year Ridgway was questioned over the disappearance of Marie Malvar. He was arrested again in 1984 for soliciting a female police officer posing as a prostitute. In the same year his truck was seen regularly cruising down the main strip. The only trouble was the police didn't have any actual evidence linking him to any of the victims. They searched his house and truck and took a saliva sample from his mouth to determine his blood type, but, in the end, nothing came of it. As a last resort, he was given a lie detector test, which he

# HE WAS GIVEN A LIE DETECTOR TEST WHICH HE PASSED

# ON 30 NOVEMBER 2001, ALMOST 20 YEARS AFTER THE CRIMES HAD BEEN COMMITTED, DAVE REICHERT ARRESTED GARY RIDGWAY

RIGHT: Virginia Graham, sister of Green River Killer victim Debra Estes speaks in court during the sentencing of Gary Ridgeway December 18, 2003.
BELOW: The Green River Killer, Gary Ridgeway faces Judge Richard A. Jones after reading a statement to the court at his trial for the murders of 48 women.

passed. The police continued to regard him as a suspect, but they had nothing on him.

After yet another setback, the investigation gradually fell apart. Bodies of women murdered between 1982 and 1984 were still occasionally being found, but, as there was nothing further to go on, the task force was disbanded. The case remained open, but with only one detective assigned to it, and no progress was made throughout the 1990s. In 2001 one of the detectives from the original task force, Dave Reichert, was elected sheriff of King County. He was not a man who believed in giving up and ordered the case to be fully reopened. A

team of detectives were appointed and they began to utilize technology not available to the original investigation. Samples of semen collected from the three bodies found in the Green River in 1982 were sent to a laboratory for DNA analysis, together with a sample of the saliva taken from Gary Ridgway in 1987. In September 2001 the lab report came back with positive matches between all the samples. On 30 November 2001, almost 20 years after the crimes had been committed, Dave Reichert arrested Gary Ridgway. He was charged with the murders of Marcia Chapman, Opal Mills and Cynthia Hinds. There was sufficient circumstantial evidence to charge him

with one additional murder and, after his arrest, forensic tests on paint he used at work linked him with three more victims.

At first Ridgway maintained his innocence. Prosecutors made it clear they would be seeking the death penalty, which was applicable in Washington State for cases involving multiple murder. Before the trial began, Ridgway's lawyers entered into plea bargaining with the prosecution, and a deal was agreed. Ridgway would confess to the Green River killings in exchange for the prosecution dropping their demand for the death penalty. The Green River case file contained details of 48 murders and Ridgway confessed to them all. He also led prosecutors to a number of the bodies of victims which had not yet been found, including that of Marie Malvar. At the trial Ridgway pleaded guilty and was sentenced to 48 life terms without the possibility of parole. He is currently serving the sentence in Walla Walla Prison, where he will remain for the rest of his life.

There can be no doubt that Gary Ridgway was the man responsible for the Green River killings, but there are some aspects of the case that do not completely add up. Some people who were involved with the case think Ridgway committed many more than 48 murders. Of the murders he was convicted of, 46 were committed between 1982 and 1984. It is widely thought that Ridgway killed more women during this period, but the bodies have never been found. The two other murders were committed in 1990 and 1998. It is hard to believe these were the only murders Ridgway committed in the 16 years he spent at liberty after 1984, until his arrest in 2001. Once serial killers have started killing, they do not suddenly stop. In all probability there are many more bodies buried around Seattle. When Ridgway was asked how many women he had killed in total, he said 'I killed so many, I have a hard time keeping them straight.'

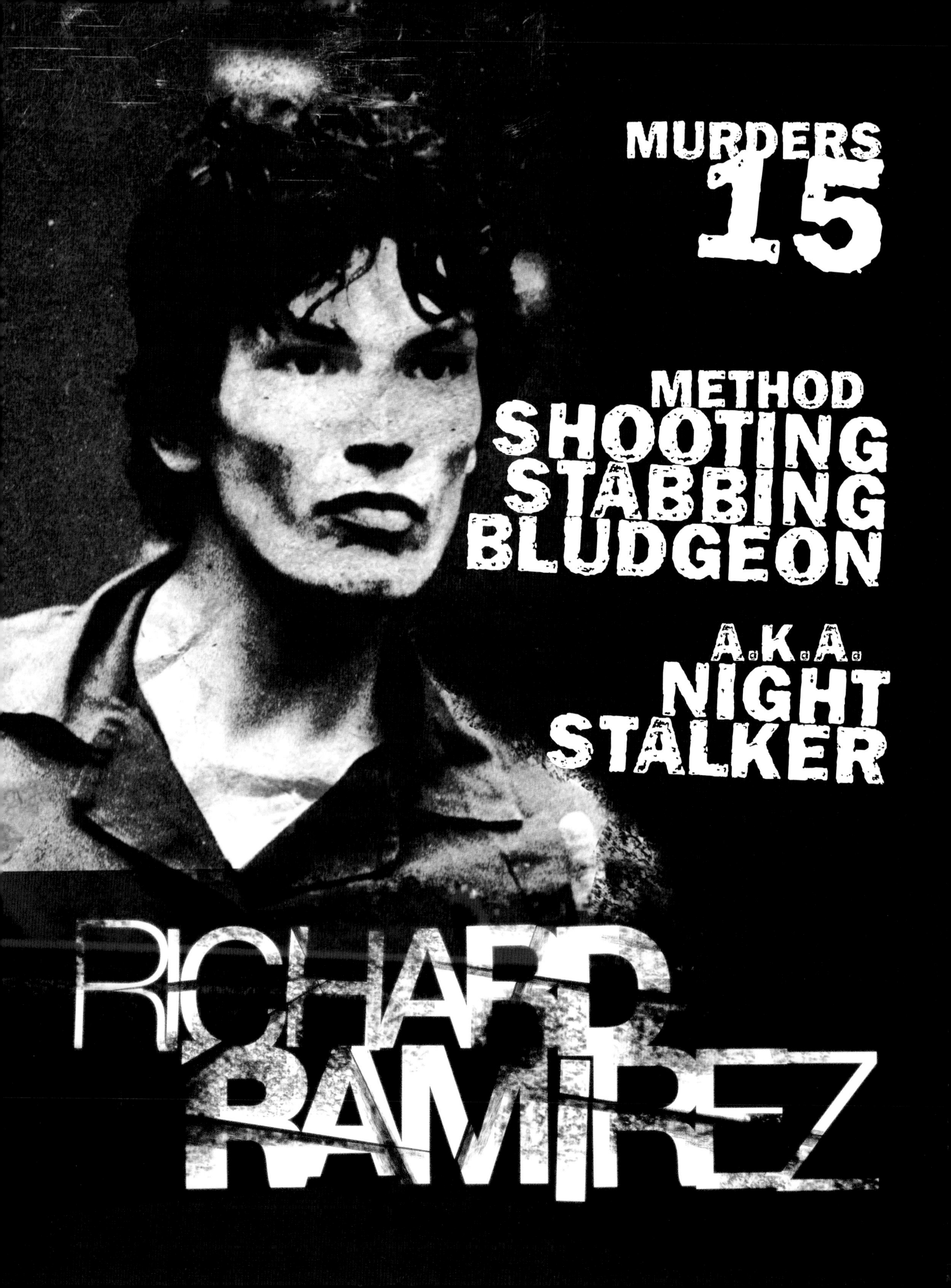

MURDERS
15

METHOD
SHOOTING
STABBING
BLUDGEON

A.K.A.
NIGHT
STALKER

RICHARD
RAMIREZ

# A tall, dark, hispanic man with acute halitosis who killed indiscriminately and without remorse – the Night Stalker sounds like a character from a bad slasher-movie, but Richard Ramirez was all too real. He rampaged his way through people's homes before scrawling satanic symbols on walls and on the bodies of his victims. In the end a simple visit to a LA drug store sealed his fate forever.

The long hot summer of 1985 was a bad time to be in Los Angeles. The number of murders in the city reached unprecedented levels and there was an epidemic of serial killings. Five different madmen were on the loose, but, even with all the carnage going on, one name stood out from the pack. The media called him the Night Stalker because he attacked at around midnight. Unlike all the other killers, he didn't target a particular group of vulnerable people. Men and women, old and young – the Night Stalker didn't differentiate. He killed them all. He broke into houses and apartments and carried out frenzied attacks on whomever he found inside. Afterwards he drew inverted pentagrams on the walls and on the bodies of his victims. It was as if he was performing a satanic ritual. The LAPD had a description of him – he was a tall Hispanic man with rotting teeth and halitosis – but they were making no progress in stopping his killing rampage. The inhabitants of the city were accustomed to the daily news of violent crime, but this was different. Nobody was safe in their beds at night.

On 24 August, the Night Stalker struck in Mission Viejo, 80 km (50 miles) south of Los Angeles. At midnight he broke into an apartment and found 29-year-old William Carns and his fiancée Inez Erickson, asleep in bed. He shot Carns in the head three times. Miraculously

Carns survived the attack, but would suffer from permanent brain damage. Then he tied Inez Erickson's wrists and ankles and subjected her to a prolonged sexual assault, forcing her to repeat '*I love Satan*' over and over again as he was raping her. After ransacking the apartment and taking anything of value he could find, he left. Erickson struggled free in time to see him drive away in an orange Toyota and called the police. The next day a local boy told them he had seen an orange Toyota driving slowly around the neighbourhood. He thought it was suspicious and wrote down some of the numbers of the licence plate. It was enough for the police to establish the car had been stolen in Los Angeles a few days before. They put out an All Points Bulletin, the APB made famous by TV cop shows, and the car was found abandoned. A forensic examination of the interior came up with a fingerprint on the rear-view mirror. The central

police computer in Sacramento matched it to the prints of a man with convictions for theft and drug offences in Texas and California. The man's name was Richard Ramirez.

On 30 August the LAPD released photographs and a detailed description of Ramirez to all the news media in California. The following day his mug shot was on the front page of every newspaper in the state. Ramirez arrived back in Los Angeles from a drug-buying trip to Phoenix, Arizona, that same day. It didn't take long for somebody to recognize him. He was in a drug store in east Los Angeles, standing next to a copy of the Spanish language newspaper *La Opinion*. His picture was on the front of it. The staff and the customers were all looking at him and pointing. He made a run for it, trying to steal a car parked in a side street. The owner was underneath it, working on the transmission, and emerged to

BELOW: Police drawing of Los Angeles Night Stalker Killer.

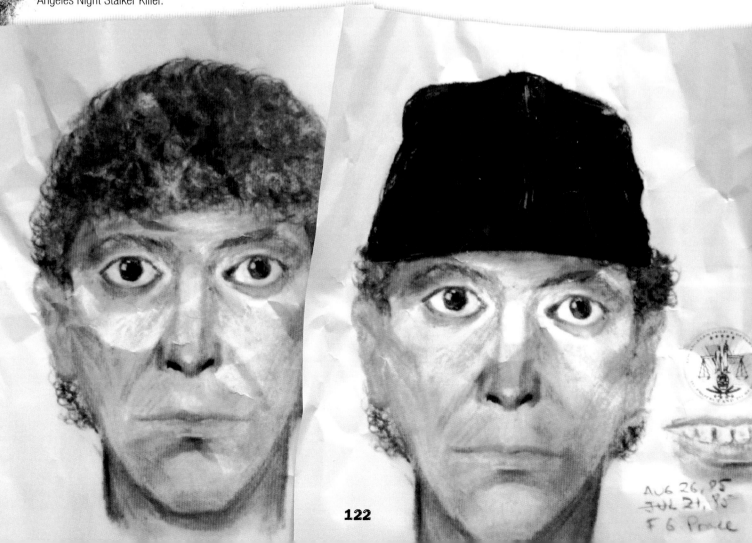

# OBSESSED WITH SATAN AND DEVIL WORSHIP

fight Ramirez off. He ran back out onto the street and tried to hijack another car. By now a crowd was building up and they chased after him, they caught him and wrestled him to the ground. He was surrounded by an angry mob and, just as it was about to turn really ugly, a police patrol car arrived. Ramirez begged the police officers to save him. They took him into custody to prevent the mob from tearing him apart.

There was nothing much in Richard Ramirez's past to suggest what he would become. He was the youngest son of a Mexican family, who moved to El Paso before he was born. After dropping out of school he took to a life of petty crime and smoking dope. In his early twenties he moved to California, but the change didn't have much effect on his lifestyle. By now he was stealing cars and breaking into houses to pay for a serious cocaine habit. It is hard to know if it was the drugs or the music he was listening to, which included lots of references to the devil and hell, but, for whatever reason, he became obsessed with Satan and devil worship.

On 28 June 1984 Ramirez crossed the line from petty criminal to murderer. He broke into the apartment of 79-year-old Jennie Vincow in Glassel Park, a suburb in north-east Los Angeles, but there was nothing worth stealing. Maybe this was what pushed him over the edge. He attacked the woman with a knife while she was sleeping, stabbing her repeatedly and slashing her throat. Before leaving he had sex with the dead body.

After that first attack, Ramirez didn't kill again for over eight months. On the night of 17 March 1985, he followed Maria Hernandez into the garage of her condo in Rosemead, on the outskirts of Los Angeles, as she returned home. As she got out of her car, he tried to shoot her in the face. By some miracle the bullet ricocheted off the car keys in her hands, as she lifted them up to defend

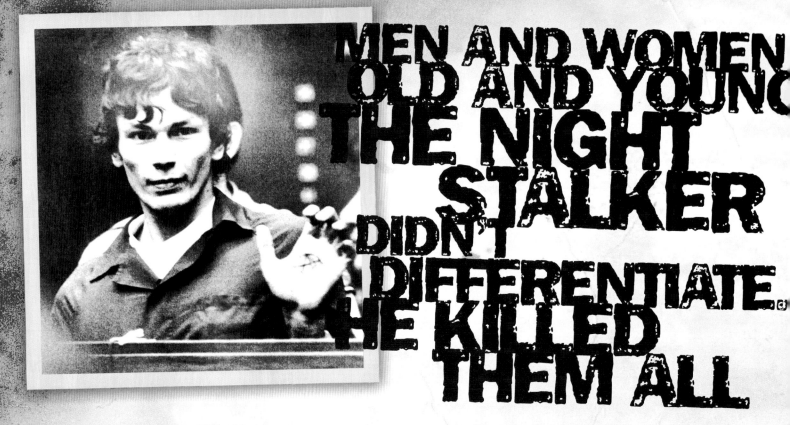

# MEN AND WOMEN OLD AND YOUNG THE NIGHT STALKER DIDN'T DIFFERENTIATE. HE KILLED THEM ALL

herself, and didn't hit her. Ramirez kicked her out of the way and went into the condo, where he shot and killed Dayle Okazaki. It was not enough to satisfy him that night. An hour later he pulled a thirty-year-old Taiwanese woman called Tsia-Lian Yu out of her car in nearby Monterey Park and shot her twice. She was alive when a police officer found her, but died before the ambulance he called arrived.

Ten days later Ramirez shot Vincent Zazarra, 64, and his wife Maxine, 44, in their house in Whittier, 20 km (12 miles) out of Los Angeles. After they were dead he stabbed Maxine Zazarra repeatedly, carving out the letter 'T' with stab wounds on her chest. Then he gouged her eyes out with the knife and took them away with him. The police now knew for sure they had a serial killer and rapist on their hands. It was six weeks before the next attack. Ramirez broke into the Monterey Park home of William and Lillie Loi, who were both in their sixties. He shot William Loi in the head, who survived just long enough to phone the police, then savagely beat Lillie Loi until she told him where to find their valuables.

A pattern was beginning to emerge. After he broke into a house, Ramirez would deal with the man first, before turning his attention to the woman. There were eight more attacks over the next three months. Ramirez raped a 44-year-old mother after he locked her son in a closet. He attacked two elderly sisters,

hitting them both over the head with a hammer and raping them. One of the sisters survived the attack, the other didn't. A few weeks later a sixteen-year-old girl also survived after he had hit her repeatedly with a crowbar. On 7 January he beat two women to death in separate attacks and, two weeks later shot an elderly couple in their house in Glendale. That same night he broke into another house in Sun Valley where he shot and killed a man as he slept and then raped the man's wife and eight-year-old son.

The attacks continued in August. Ramirez shot Christopher and Virginia Petersen in the head as they were sleeping in their house in Northridge. Both survived and Christopher Petersen, with a bullet lodged in his brain, chased Ramirez out of the house. Two days later he killed 35-year-old Ahmed Zia and brutally raped Suu Kyi Zia in Diamond Bar. She described her attacker to the police. He was a tall thin Hispanic man, with a rank body odour and breath so bad it almost made her sick.

Ramirez took a trip to San Francisco after the attack in Diamond Bar. He broke into Peter and Barbara Pan's home, shooting both of them in the head. Peter was killed instantly, but Barbara Pan survived and gave the police an accurate description of the Night Stalker. Ramirez then returned to Los Angeles, committing the attack on William Carns and Inez Erickson that would lead to him being caught in east Los Angeles.

The police charged Ramirez with 14 counts of murder. There were more than 40 other charges, mostly of attempted murder and rape, not including the attacks in San Francisco. The trial process became one of the longest in American history. The defence came up with a bewildering number of methods to delay the start. They wanted to have the location of the trial moved and the judge replaced. If nothing else worked, one of the defence lawyers would say they were sick, which would halt proceedings until he recovered. Jury selection didn't begin until three years after the arrest and then went on for more than six months. Eventually, after almost 1600 potential jurors had been interviewed, a jury was selected and the trial finally began.

The trial descended into farce on a number of occasions, particularly when a rumour started that Ramirez was planning to have a gun smuggled into the court so he could shoot the prosecutor. Ramirez attracted lots of female admirers, who came to the courtroom dressed in black every day and wrote hundreds of letters to him in prison. More than 100 witnesses took the stand and 521 exhibits were presented to the court. The trial was becoming a circus. Eventually the jury retired to consider the mountain of evidence. One of the jurors was murdered during the process and was replaced by a very frightened reserve, even though the murderer had been caught and had nothing to do with Ramirez. On 20 September 1989 they finally returned a guilty verdict on 13 charges of murder and 30 related felonies. A few weeks later Ramirez was sentenced to death in the San Quentin gas chamber. As he was led from the court he said to reporters, 'Big deal. Death always went with the territory. I'll see you in Disneyland.'

Richard Ramirez is still on death row in San Quentin, almost 20 years after he was sentenced. In 1996 he married one of the women who had been writing to him since the trial. Despite the evidence against him she claims he is innocent and misunderstood, and says she will commit suicide if he is executed. Her unshakable loyalty to him is almost as hard to understand as what motivated Ramirez to commit such terrible crimes in the first place.

OPPOSITE PAGE: Richard Ramirez flashes his left palm showing a pentagram, a symbol of satanic worship, after he was replaced by 2 new attorneys.
BELOW: Richard Ramirez leaving a police station flanked by officers 31 August 1985.

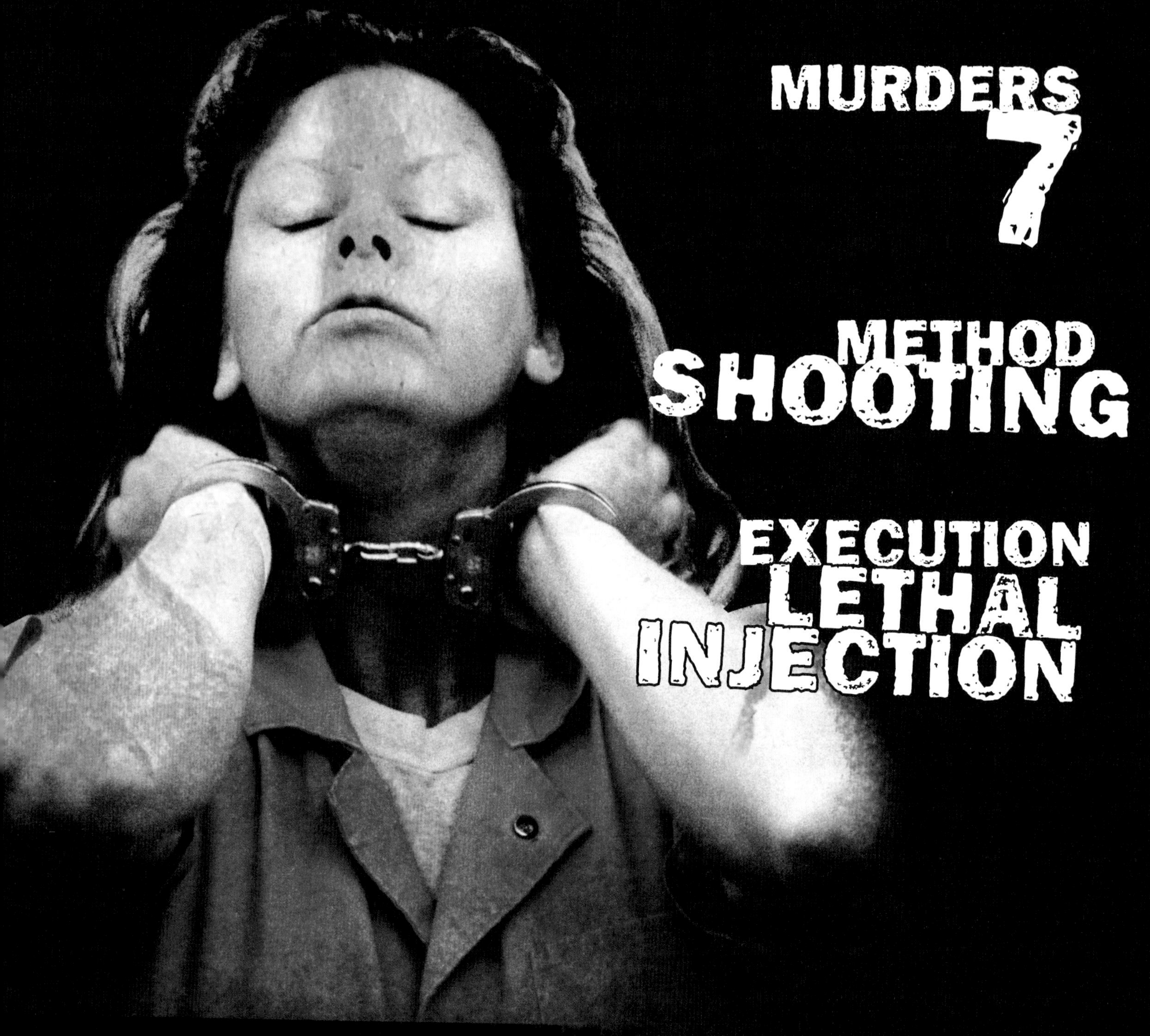

MURDERS
7

METHOD
SHOOTING

EXECUTION
LETHAL
INJECTION

AILEEN
WUORNOS

# Aileen Wuornos killed the men who had paid to have sex with her, claiming to have been a victim of sexual violence acting in self defence. But was she? Or, as was claimed at her trial, was Wuornos simply attempting to steal from her victims in order to keep herself and her lover off the breadline?

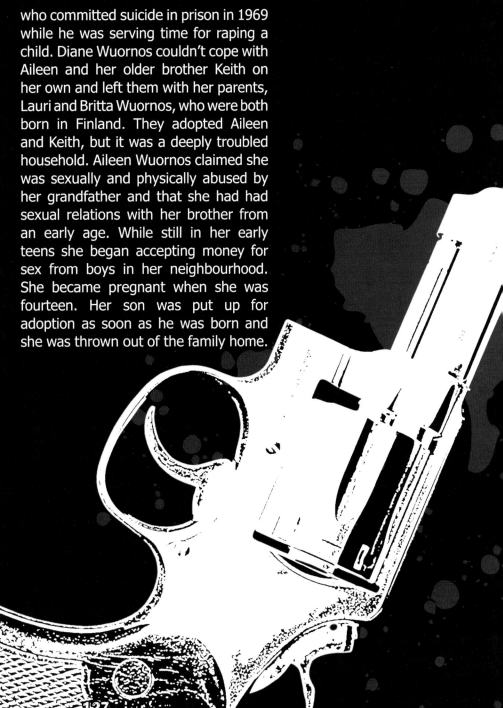

Prostitutes have regularly been the target of male serial killers. Aileen Wuornos was a prostitute, but she was different – she was the killer not the victim. But she was not the first female serial killer, as all the frenzied news media reports at the time claimed she was. Although a rare phenomenon, there have certainly been women who killed multiple times before Wuornos did. The difference was the way Wuornos killed her victims. Almost without exception women killers murder people they know: husbands, lovers, patients and, sometimes, their own children. Aileen Wuornos didn't do that. She behaved much more like a male serial killer would. Between November 1989 and November 1990, she shot seven of her 'Johns', as she called the men who paid to have sex with her, in cold blood. After she was caught, Wuornos claimed she was acting in self-defence, but there can be little doubt that her prime motivation for killing was money.

Aileen Wuornos was born in Rochester, Michigan, in 1956. To say she had a difficult upbringing would be a huge understatement. Her father, Leo Pitman, left Diane Wuornos, her mother, before Aileen was born. He was a paedophile

who committed suicide in prison in 1969 while he was serving time for raping a child. Diane Wuornos couldn't cope with Aileen and her older brother Keith on her own and left them with her parents, Lauri and Britta Wuornos, who were both born in Finland. They adopted Aileen and Keith, but it was a deeply troubled household. Aileen Wuornos claimed she was sexually and physically abused by her grandfather and that she had had sexual relations with her brother from an early age. While still in her early teens she began accepting money for sex from boys in her neighbourhood. She became pregnant when she was fourteen. Her son was put up for adoption as soon as he was born and she was thrown out of the family home.

From then on she made money from prostitution and theft, picking up a criminal record for a string of petty offences. After leaving school, Wuornos left Michigan, hitchhiking from state to state and turning tricks in order to eat. She returned to Michigan occasionally to see her brother, until he died of throat cancer in 1976 at the age of 21.

By the early 1980s Wuornos was living in Florida. She served time in prison a number of times, for armed robbery and for passing stolen checks. In 1986 she met Tyria Moore in a gay bar in Daytona Beach, the beginning of a relationship which would continue, off and on, for five years. Wuornos supported them with the money she made through prostitution and by pawning whatever she could steal. She picked up men in bars and at truck stops and, so she said, carried a gun after she was attacked on a number of occasions by her clients. By 1989 Wuornos and Moore were constantly running short of money. They were having trouble making the rent and, when they couldn't, ended up sleeping rough. Wuornos was afraid Moore would leave if the situation didn't improve. What she needed was a new way of making money.

The first victim was 51-year old Richard Mallory. His abandoned car was found near Daytona Beach, Florida, on 31 November 1989. Two weeks later, his body was found dumped in woodland north of the city. He had been shot three times with a .22 handgun. An investigation revealed he was well known to the prostitutes of the Daytona area. The police initially focused their attention on a stripper who went by the stage name of Chastity, but, after they eliminated her from the investigation, the case went cold.

AT FIRST THE POLICE REFUSED TO ACKNOWLEDGE THEY WERE DEALING WITH A SERIAL KILLER, BUT AS THE KILLING SPREE CONTINUED, THEY HAD NO OTHER CHOICE THAN TO ACCEPT WHAT WAS STARING THEM IN THE FACE

There were no similar murders in Florida until 1 June 1990, when the body of David Spears, was discovered in woodland in Citrus County, 65 km (40 miles) north of Tampa. He had been missing for ten days and was found shot six times with a .22. The following day his truck was reported abandoned by the side of Interstate 75. On 6 June the naked body of Charles Carskaddon was found near Tampa. His killer had shot him nine times with the same .22 gun. At first the police refused to acknowledge they were dealing with a serial killer, but, as the killing spree continued, they had no other choice than to accept what was staring them in the face. Tyria Moore's sister, it turned out, had come to stay with her from Pennsylvania. Aileen Wuornos thought Tyria was planning to go back to Pennsylvania with her sister and needed to make some money

quickly so she could persuade Tyria to stay with her.

Peter Siems, 65, went missing on 7 June. He left his home in Palm Beach to visit relatives in Arkansas, but was never seen again. A month later a woman watched from her house as a Pontiac Sunbird careered off the road near Orange Springs, crashing through some undergrowth before jolting to a stop. Two women got out of the car, arguing with each other. One of them had hurt her arm, but refused an offer of help. They didn't want the woman to call the police or an ambulance and walked away, saying they lived nearby. She called the police anyway and they established that the car belonged to Peter Siems. A police artist drew up a sketch from the description the woman gave him. One of the women was quite tall with blonde hair and a freckled face, and the other was smaller and had brown hair. The police didn't know it at the time, but it was an accurate description of Aileen Wuornos and Tyria Moore. Over the next few months three more men were killed in almost identical circumstances as the previous four victims had been.

By September the sketch of the women seen leaving Peter Siems' car had been widely circulated around Florida. The same names were coming up in connection with it time and again. The

OPPOSITE PAGE: 51-year-old video repair shop owner Richard Mallory was the first of seven victims of Aileen Wuornos. BELOW: The Last Resort Bar where Aileen Wuornos was arrested for the murders of seven men.

name of the brown-haired woman was Tyria Moore. The blonde woman was using a number of aliases, including Lee Blahovec, Lori Grody and Cammie Marsh Green. Detectives followed their trail through a number of motels and apartments without catching up with them. In December they began checking pawn shops in Daytona and found items pawned by Cammie Marsh Greene in one of them. There was a camera and a radar detector they could trace back to Richard Mallory. A fingerprint on the pawn shop receipt was matched to a woman who had criminal records in Michigan and Colorado as well as Florida. The police now had the name of the other woman – Aileen Wuornos.

On 9 January 1991 the police caught up with Wuornos in a bar called The Last Resort in Port Orange. She was arrested and denied anything to do with the seven murders. Tyria Moore was picked up at her sister's house in Pittston, Pennsylvania, the following day. She was sent back to Florida and offered a deal. If she could get Wuornos to confess, she would not have to face any charges herself. Over the course of three days Moore phoned Wuornos in prison several times, telling Wuornos if she didn't confess the police were going to charge her, Moore, with the murders as well. On 16 January Wuornos confessed to six of the murders, denying she had killed Peter Siems.

Wuornos was put on trial for the murder of Richard Mallory in January 1992. By this time a born-again Christian called Arlene Pralle was championing her cause. Pralle said she had been told to do so in a dream and, during the trial, she and her husband legally adopted Wuornos. They would fall out later when Wuornos accused Pralle of only becoming involved in the first place to make money out of the publicity the case had generated. She was not the

# AFTER THREE 15 MINUTE INTERVIEWS, WUORNOS WAS DECLARED MENTALLY FIT TO BE EXECUTED

RIGHT: Aileen Wuornos testifies during her murder trial in 1992.

only one, detectives, attorneys and witnesses were all approached by film and publishing agents, while the trial continued, with offers to buy their stories. It was seriously prejudicial to the outcome of the trial. Should Wuornos be found not guilty, there would be no story to sell.

During the trial Wuornos was the only witness for the defence and did herself few favours in the witness box. She contradicted herself on a number of occasions and directed angry and foul-mouthed tirades at the prosecutor and jury. Wuornos claimed Mallory had violently attacked and raped her and she had shot him in self-defence. Details of the other murder charges were introduced by the prosecution, which, unlike almost every other state, was allowed in Florida. It seriously undermined Wuornos's claim of self-defence. The jury took less than two hours to find Wuornos guilty of murder, and she was sentenced to death. Almost a year later a journalist discovered that Richard Mallory had served ten years in prison in another state for aggravated rape. Although this information was obviously pertinent to Wuornos's defence, she was refused a retrial and the sentence was allowed to stand.

Wuornos pleaded guilty to five other murders and was sentenced to death on each count. She was not charged with the murder of Peter Siems as his body had not been found. A lengthy appeals process began, which continued until 2001. At this point Wuornos decided she wanted to die. She petitioned the Florida Supreme Court to prevent any more appeals. Jeb Bush, the Governor of Florida, ordered psychiatric reports to be compiled and, after three 15 minute interviews, Wuornos was declared mentally fit to be executed. On 9 October 2002 she was put to death by lethal injection in Florida State Prison.

Nick Bloomfield, a British documentary film-maker, has made two films about Wuornos. The first, *Aileen Wuornos: The Selling of a Serial Killer*, concerns the attempts by all parties to cash in on the publicity surrounding the case, and the second, *Aileen: Life and Death of a Serial Killer*, documents Wuornos's declining mental state in the months before her execution. Bloomfield has said since that he considers the decision to execute her to be highly questionable.

The Hollywood film *Monster*, starring Charlize Theron as Wuornos, was released in 2003. For the role Theron, considered by many to be one of the most beautiful actresses in Hollywood, gained 14 kg (30 lbs) in weight and wore heavy make-up and prosthetic teeth in order to resemble Aileen Wuornos. She won an Oscar for the portrayal, picking up the award on what would have been Wuornos's 48th birthday.

BELOW: Sidney Bertisch of Gainesville, Florida protests against the execution by lethal injection of Aileen Wuornos on 9 October 2002.

131

MURDERS
7

METHOD
SHOOTING
STABBING

SENTENCE
LIFE
IMPRISONMENT

IVAN
MILAT

Ivan Milat belonged to a family whose very name meant **violence and murder** to the people of the agricultural community where they lived. **Backpackers were disappearing** on the Hume Highway, only to reappear having been used as **target practice for a psychopath** with a Ruger .22 rifle. It didn't take long for locals to finger Milat as the killer, but was it really him?

The Belango State Forest is an extensive pine plantation owned by the New South Wales Government. It is a few miles off the Hume Highway, between Sydney and Canberra, and is an area of free access to the public. On 19 September 1992 two men on an orienteering run through the forest stopped at a control point on their map. It was a large boulder near a prominent landmark called Executioner's Drop — the sheer rock face of a wooded valley. The smell by the boulder was terrible. One of them thought an animal, possibly a kangaroo or wallaby, must have died nearby and was about to move on when his companion called him over to a mound of branches and decaying leaves. They could see some hair and part of a T-shirt sticking out of the mound and the heel of a shoe was protruding from one end. They ran out of the forest and contacted the police at Bowral, the nearest town in the Southern Highlands of New South Wales.

The police recovered the partially decomposed body of a young woman. She had been stabbed repeatedly in the chest and neck with a single-bladed knife. The following day a search of the immediate area revealed the body of a second young woman not far from the first. An autopsy would show she had been stabbed and then shot ten times in the head from three different angles. It looked as if the killer had used the body for target practice. It didn't take long to establish the identities of the two women. They were Joanne Walters and Caroline Clarke, both 22-year-old British backpackers. They had left the Kings Cross district of Sydney together in April of that year, saying they were going to head south to

ABOVE: Murder victims left to right: Deborah Everest, Simone Schmidl, Anja Habschied, Joanne Walters, Gabor Neugebauer, James Gibson and Caroline Clarke.

OPPOSITE PAGE: Court officials visit the Belanglo Forest, south of Sydney, where the bodies of seven backpackers were found in the early 1990s.

look for work, and had not been heard from since. Forensic scientists couldn't be sure, but they thought that both women had been sexually assaulted.

Further searches in Belango State Forest recovered spent cartridge shells from an American-made Ruger .22 rifle. A forensic psychiatrist visited the scene of the murders and said he thought they were not opportunist attacks. The murders had been pre-planned and carried out by more than one person. The murderers, he said, would have been familiar with the surroundings and probably lived locally. After completing an extensive search through the rest of the forest, New South Wales Police announced it was an isolated incident and no more bodies were likely to be found. Unfortunately they were wrong.

Over the following year the investigation stalled completely. In October 1993 a man collecting firewood in the forest found some bones he thought might be human. Another search discovered two bodies hidden in the brush. Both had been killed in exactly the same way as the previous two victims. They proved to be two 19-year-old Australians, Deborah Everist and James Gibson, who had gone missing from Victoria in 1989. Within

days three more bodies were found. They were all German backpackers. Simone Schmidl, 20, had gone missing in January 1991 and the young couple Gabor Neugebauer, 21, and Anja Habschied, 20, in December 1991. It looked as if Anja Habschied had been decapitated with a single blow from a large blade, possibly a sword. More bullets from a .22 Ruger were found in the immediate vicinity of the bodies. At a press conference the police announced what everyone already knew – there was a serial killer, or killers, targeting young travellers on the Hume Highway. The police were frantically going through records of backpackers who had gone missing in Australia. Although there were a number of other missing people, no more bodies were found.

A public appeal for information brought a huge response. The names of several members of the Milat family, who lived in the area, kept coming up. Several people told the police they should talk to Ivan Milat, who was said to be obsessed with guns. The police interviewed him but, with no direct evidence, there was not much else they could do.

As soon as Paul Onions heard reports of the murders he phoned the police hotline from his home in the UK. He told a detective from the investigation he had been hitchhiking along the Hume Highway in 1990 and had accepted a lift from a man driving a pickup who pulled a gun on him. Onions escaped from the pickup and ran, with the man firing shots at his back. He reported the attack to the police at Bowral, but heard no more about it. It was obviously important information, but details of the call were lost in the huge amounts of information being received. It would be five months before the New South Wales Police got back to him. In April 1994 they flew him over to Australia and he picked Ivan Milat out of photographs shown to him.

It was enough for the police to get warrants to search Milat's house. They found items of clothing and camping equipment belonging to some of the victims and parts of a Ruger .22 rifle hidden in the roof cavity of the garage. Milat was arrested and immediately claimed he was being set up by other members of his family. Forensic tests on the rifle matched it to the bullets found at the site of the killings, and an examination of Milat's employment records also connected him to the crimes. In searches of the houses of other members of the Milat family, the police recovered more items belonging to the victims. A sword was found in a locked cupboard at the house of Ivan Milat's mother.

Milat was charged with the seven murders and the attempted murder of Paul Onions. He stuck to his story that two of his brothers were trying to frame him. The weight of evidence against him personally was overwhelming, and the jury found him guilty on all charges. He was sentenced to seven life terms for the murders and six years for the attempted murder of Onions. To this day Milat maintains his innocence. The New South Wales Police think he could well have committed many more murders and may well have been helped by at least one of his brothers. So far they have not been able to establish any links to other missing people in Australia. In 2005 a journalist asked one of Milat's brothers if Ivan had been responsible for more than seven murders. He said people had gone missing wherever Ivan had been and thought he had killed at least 20 more people.

**MURDERS 17**

**METHOD STRANGLE**

**A.K.A. THE MILWAUKEE CANNIBAL**

# JEFFREY DAHMER

**Jeffrey Dahmer was allowed to kill and kill again because he was white and polite, and because the police preferred to keep their distance from the domestic affairs of gay men. If the cops had meddled just a little more, they may have revealed the sick crimes of this monstrous killer much sooner.**

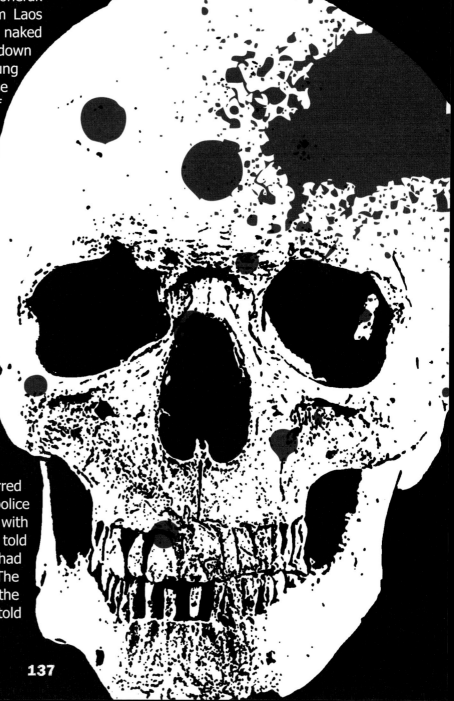

In the early hours of 27 May 1991 Konerak Simthasomphone, a fourteen-year-old boy from Laos who didn't speak much English, was found naked and disorientated in the street in a run-down neighbourhood of Milwaukee. The two young women who found him could not get any sense out of him, but they could tell he was terrified of something. They called the police and, by the time they arrived, a man was trying to talk the boy into coming back to an apartment with him. He told the police officers the boy was his 19-year-old boyfriend and had got drunk after they had had a row. The man was polite and reasonable and he showed the officers ID, which gave his name as Jeffrey Dahmer. He was also white, unlike the two young women who had called the police. They told the officers that, before they arrived, the man had been trying to drag the boy away against his will. The officers accepted Dahmer's story, ignored the protests of the young women, and accompanied the man and boy back to an apartment block on North 24th Street. After a few minutes the officers decided they had better things to do than to get involved in a domestic dispute between two gay men, and so they left.

Two months later a similar incident occurred not far from the same apartment block. Two police officers found a young black man in the street with a pair of handcuffs dangling from one wrist. He told them about a 'weird dude' in an apartment who had drugged him and tried to stab him with a knife. The officers went to the apartment and knocked on the door. A 31-year-old blond man opened it and told

# IN THE BEDROOM THE OFFICER FOUND PHOTOGRAPHS OF DEAD AND DISMEMBERED BODIES. ONE OF THE PHOTOGRAPHS SHOWED A SKULL IN A FRIDGE

them his name was Jeffrey Dahmer. He was embarrassed about the disturbance and said he would get the key for the handcuffs from the bedroom. One of the officers went with him. In the bedroom the officer found photographs of dead and dismembered bodies. One of the photographs showed a skull in a fridge.

After a struggle the officers handcuffed Dahmer and, with him subdued, one of them opened the fridge door. A face stared back out at him. He slammed the door and shouted to his partner that there was a severed head in the refrigerator. It was only the start. There were three more heads in plastic bags in the freezer along with various cuts of meat which, when examined, proved to be human. Elsewhere in the apartment there was a cooking pot with human hands and a penis in it and a barrel of acid containing the remains of four young men. Dahmer was arrested and soon confessed to the murder of 17 people.

Konerak Simthasomphone was one of the victims. After the police had escorted him back to Dahmer's apartment and left him there, Dahmer strangled him and had sex with the corpse. Photographs found in the apartment showed the dismembered body. Dahmer kept the skull, boiling the flesh off it and keeping it as a souvenir. It emerged that when the police were in the apartment, the body of another of Dahmer's victims was in the bedroom. Had they checked Dahmer's background, they would have found he had been arrested in 1988 for molesting Simthasomphone's brother, for which he was given a one-year prison sentence with five years' probation.

Details of the police officer's radio conversation with their dispatcher were later made public. They made homophobic comments and joked about reuniting the lovers. Both officers were dismissed from the Milwaukee Police Department, but were later reinstated on appeal. The black community of Milwaukee were outraged at the behaviour of the police officers. There appeared to be a racial element to their actions in ignoring two black women and accepting what a white man said. The majority of Dahmer's victims were young black men and, for a few days, the city was on the edge of erupting into race riots. Gradually the city calmed down again, but nobody could forget the horror of what had gone on in Dahmer's apartment.

Jeffrey Dahmer was born in Milwaukee in 1960, but moved to rural Ohio with his parents when he was six years old. There is very little in his childhood that could explain what was to come. He was a relatively normal and happy boy. Quite early on he exhibited an unusual fascination with the bodies of dead animals, but he does not appear to have killed or mutilated any himself. His parents' marriage was a troubled one and he was jealous of his younger brother, who was born in 1966, but, again, these are hardly unusual circumstances. Lionel Dahmer, Jeffrey's father, has spoken of feeling as though he gradually lost his son from the age of six onwards, but he, like everyone else, could not explain what led Dahmer down the dark road he ended up on.

By the time Dahmer was eighteen his mother and father had separated and were involved in a bitter divorce battle. He was left on his own in the family home over the summer and, on 18 June 1978, picked up a nineteen-year-old hitchhiker called Steven Hicks. Dahmer invited Hicks back to the house for a drink and, when Hicks said he wanted to leave, an argument started. Dahmer

hit Hicks over the head with a dumb-bell and, with Hicks unconscious, strangled him to death. He dragged the body into the crawl space under the house and dismembered it. At first he buried the remains in the back yard. When the smell of decomposing flesh became noticeable, Dahmer dug up the body parts and smashed the bones to pieces with a sledgehammer, before scattering them in nearby woodland.

Later that year Dahmer went to Ohio State University. He was kicked out in his first year because of his drinking, which was escalating towards alcoholism. His father talked him in to joining the army.

ABOVE: Portrait of Tony Hughes, murder victim of Jeffrey Dahmer.
OPPOSITE PAGE: The front exterior of the Oxford Apartments where Jeffrey Dahmer was arrested in July 1991.

After 18 months he was discharged due to alcoholism, which was leading to aggressive behaviour. After a brief spell of hiding from his family in Florida, in 1982 he moved into the basement apartment of his grandmother's house in Milwaukee. At first he appeared to be straightening himself out. He got a job in a chocolate factory and his family must have thought he was trying to put his troubles behind him. But there were signs that everything was not quite right. He was arrested twice for exposing himself in public, and allegations were made against him by a man saying Dahmer had spiked his drink with crushed up sleeping pills and tried to rob him. With no evidence to go on, the police didn't charge Dahmer.

In November 1987 Dahmer killed for the second time. He had been frequenting the gay bars and bath houses of Milwaukee for a number of years and met 25-year-old Steven Toumi in one of them. At the end of the night they went to a hotel together and, at some point, Dahmer strangled Toumi. Initially Dahmer didn't know what to do with the body. He decided to take it back to his apartment and went out to buy a suitcase large enough to accommodate the body. Once he was in his apartment, he had sex with the body, cut it up and disposed of it in the garbage.

Over the next four years there would be four more victims, although Dahmer had learned from his mistake with Steven Toumi. From then on he invited the people he would kill back to his apartment. In the summer of 1988 his grandmother asked him to find an apartment of his own. She was tired of the noise he made at night when he invited his male friends back to his place for a drink – the music would go on into the early hours. She also complained to him about the smell, which, he explained, was caused by the animals he skinned in the garage.

In September 1988 Dahmer found an apartment on North 25th Street. On his first night there he enticed Keison Simthasomphone, Konerak's brother, into the apartment and spiked his drink. Keison escaped from the apartment and the incident would lead to Dahmer being arrested for second-degree sexual assault. On 25 March 1989, while he was out on bail, Dahmer killed 24-year-old Anthony Sears. After having sex with the body, he disposed of it as before, except, this time, he kept the head. He boiled it up, stripped the flesh off it and painted the skull grey – so it resembled a plastic model.

In May of that year he began his sentence for the sexual assault. He was allowed out of prison during the day so he didn't lose his job, but had no more opportunities to kill until the following year. In June 1990 he met Raymond Smith, in a gay bar. Dahmer offered Smith money to come back to his apartment and pose for some photographs. Smith agreed and, once in the apartment, accepted a drink

BELOW: A newspaper vending machine sporting the *Milwaukee Sentinel* on 29 November 1994.
OPPOSITE PAGE: Police mug shot following Jeffrey Dahmer's 1982 arrest at the Wisconsin State Fair for indecent exposure.

Milwaukee **Sentinel**

TUESDAY MORNING · NOVEMBER 29, 1994 · · · · FINAL

# Death wish realized: Inmate kills Dahmer

'It doesn't matter, Mom,' Dahmer said

Suspect is man imprisoned for '90 city murder

from Dahmer. It was drugged and, when Smith was sufficiently incapacitated, Dahmer strangled him. He added the skull to his growing collection.

From then on Dahmer went into a killing frenzy. Up until his arrest in July 1991 there would be eleven more victims. Dahmer took photographs as he hung their bodies from the shower rail over the bath and gutted them. He began to cook and eat some of the flesh he stripped off the skeletons and began to conduct gruesome experiments on them. On a number of occasions he attempted to turn his victims into zombies before killing them. After they were drugged and unconscious, he drilled a hole in their skulls and injected muriatic acid into their brains. On all but one occasion this resulted in the immediate death of the victim. In his confession Dahmer said one had survived for a few days in a zombie-like state before dying.

After his arrest Dahmer was charged with 15 murders, although he actually said he killed 17 people. The trial began on 20 June 1992 and he pleaded not guilty by reason of insanity. The defence attempted to convince the jury that no sane man would have engaged in necrophilia and cannibalism as Dahmer had. They went through all the gruesome details of the murders, but the jury agreed with the prosecution, who argued that Dahmer was a habitual liar and manipulator who knew exactly what he was doing. He was sentenced to 15 consecutive life terms in prison, giving a total of 957 years.

Dahmer only served two years of his sentence. On the morning of 28 November 1994 he and another white prisoner where left alone on a work detail with the black inmate Christopher Scarver. It was well known in the prison that Dahmer's victims had almost all been black and Scarver, who had been diagnosed as a delusional schizophrenic, took the opportunity to batter him and the other prisoner to death. Speculation that prison officers colluded in the murders by intentionally leaving Dahmer with Scarver, knowing what would happen, has never been proved.

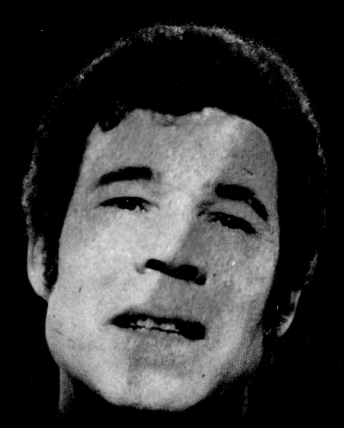

# MURDERS 12

## METHOD
# STRANGLE

## VICTIMS
# YOUNG
# WOMEN

# FRED&ROSE
# WEST

The Wests, like the Moors Murderers, relied on shared **indulgence in rape and murder** to keep the flame of their passion alive. All couples need to have something in common. Fred and Rose had the murders of at least **12 women,** including 2 of their own daughters. When 25 Cromwell Street was finally searched and the story broke, the Wests' exploits **shocked and sickened** the British public.

In August 1992 rumours about Fred and Rosemary West reached the police. The rumours accused them of sexually assaulting one of their daughters, and the police, who were well acquainted with the couple, took the matter seriously enough to get a warrant to search their house at 25 Cromwell Street, Gloucester. They found an extensive collection of pornography, home-made as well as commercial, and all sorts of equipment for use in bondage and sadomasochistic sex. They also found enough evidence to arrest both Fred and Rosemary. Fred West was charged with four counts of rape against two of his daughters and Rosemary West was charged with being his accomplice. At the trial both of the children involved refused to speak against their parents, resulting in the case being dismissed. But the police were not finished with the West family yet. They were interested in the whereabouts of another one of their daughters, who had not been seen since 1987, when she was 16.

Fred West was not at home on 24 February 1994 when the police knocked on the door of his house at 25 Cromwell Street for a second time. His twenty-year-old son Stephen opened the door and called to his mother that the police had a warrant to search the garden. They were looking for the missing daughter, Heather West. She had, according to Fred, left home after a row and was either working in a holiday camp in Devon or had changed her identity and was a prostitute somewhere in the Middle East. There was a family joke saying she was buried under the patio in the garden. Now the police had come to dig up the garden. They were not treating it as a joke.

Rosemary West phoned Fred at the building site where he was working. She told him what the police were doing and that he had better come home. It was a 20-minute drive, but it was more than four hours before he arrived. He came up with a story about falling asleep after inhaling paint fumes at work. It was the first in a long line of unlikely stories he would tell the police. What he was really doing during those four hours remains a mystery, but it seems likely that he was disposing of incriminating evidence.

## THERE WAS A FAMILY JOKE SAYING HEATHER WAS BURIED UNDER THE PATIO IN THE GARDEN.

Fred and Rosemary West met in 1968, when he was 28 and she was 15. He had already been married once and had two daughters with his first wife. Rosemary West became pregnant the following year and gave birth to Heather while Fred was serving a prison sentence for numerous counts of theft. By this time she was already working as a prostitute and brought her clients back to their house in Gloucester. They were married in 1972 and moved to a larger house in Cromwell Street because the family was growing rapidly – altogether there would be six children, not including the two from Fred's previous marriage, although two of them were fathered by Rosemary West's clients. Having a larger house was better for the prostitution business and they could also let out the spare rooms to lodgers. That year seventeen-year-old Caroline Owens came to work for them as a live-in nanny. She was propositioned by both Fred and Rosemary West and, when she rejected them both and tried to leave, she was raped. Her mother reported the attack to the police and Fred West was arrested. He claimed the sex was consensual and was let off with a fine. It appears that Fred and Rosemary decided not to give any of their future victims the opportunity of going to the police.

The search of the garden in Cromwell Street didn't come up with anything on the first day. The police left Fred and Rosemary West in the house for the night, where they no doubt discussed what story they were going to tell should anything turn up in the garden. The next day the police lifted the patio and found some bones, which a pathologist said were human and female. Fred West immediately confessed to the murder of his daughter, saying they had had a row and he had accidentally killed her. Then he let himself down by saying he had strangled her to make sure she was dead before cutting the body up and burying it. Within minutes he retracted his confession. Heather, he said, was in Bahrain. By then the pathologist had identified bones from three different legs. West changed his story again. Now he confessed to killing Heather and two other young women. He said he had killed Shirley Robinson in June 1978 and Alison Chambers in September 1979. The police arrested him for the three murders. He was adamant that his wife didn't know anything. Although the police didn't believe him, they didn't arrest Rosemary West at that time.

ABOVE: Portrait of serial killers Fred and Rose West.

The search moved inside the house. The remains of five young women, aged between 15 and 21, were found buried in small pits in the floor of the cellar. One more body was found in a similar pit in the bathroom floor. The victims were mostly lodgers or young women the Wests had employed as nannies. All were killed between April 1973 and April 1975 and, although some had been reported missing, none had been traced to Cromwell Street. The pathologist found that Fred West had cut the fingers and toes off all the

bodies and, in a few cases, the kneecaps of some of them as well. The body count was now up to nine. Fred West confessed to all the murders and, again, he said his wife had nothing to do with any of them.

No more bodies were found in the house. The police widened the search to include places where the Wests had lived previously. They were looking for Fred West's first wife, Catherine, and the eldest of the couple's two daughters, Charmaine – neither had been seen since 1971. They began to search in Much Marcle, the village in Herefordshire where Fred West was born, about 24 km (15 miles) west of Gloucester. Knowing the police were on the trail, West admitted to killing Catherine and Charmaine. His first wife was buried in a field in Much Marcle, and his daughter in the house he had lived in in Gloucester before moving to Cromwell Street. He also admitted to the murder of Anna McFall in August 1967. She was buried in another field in Much Marcle. Although the police were sure he was also responsible for the disappearance of fifteen-year-old Mary Bastholm in January 1968, he emphatically denied having anything to do with it.

By now Fred West's story of Rosemary not knowing anything about any of the murders was beginning to become untenable. Fred West was serving a prison sentence when Charmaine West had gone missing. A far more likely story was that Rosemary West had killed Charmaine on her own, and Fred had disposed of the

body after he was released from prison. Two months after Fred West's arrest, Rosemary was also taken into custody. A joint hearing was held later that year. It was the first time the couple had seen each other since Fred had been arrested. Rosemary West would not speak to her husband, saying the sight of him made her sick. At the hearing Fred West was charged with 12 murders and Rosemary West with 10. He wrote to her on a number of occasions afterwards, but she continued to refuse to have anything more to do with him. At about 1pm on 1 January 1995, while the prison warders were having lunch, Fred West hanged himself in his cell with torn up strips of bedlinen.

The evidence against Rosemary West was almost entirely circumstantial. At her trial, beginning on 3 October 1995, she continued to maintain that she knew nothing about the murders. The prosecution asked the court how this could possibly be true, since there was photographic and video evidence showing her participating in the sexual assaults of the victims. Some of the most damning testimony came from Janet Leach, who had sat in on the police interviews with Fred West as a witness and been traumatized by what she had heard. In a private conversation, he told her that Rosemary West had been involved in all the murders he committed after they first met in 1968 and had killed two of the victims on her own. Going through the details of what West had said to her again proved to be another highly traumatic experience for Leach. After she finished, she suffered a stroke and was taken to hospital.

The prosecution presented Rosemary West as the instigator and planner of the crimes. She helped Fred West lure women into the house and participated in sadistic torture sessions which, on occasion, went on for up to a week before the victim was finally killed. The defence put Rosemary West on the stand to give evidence. She gave the impression of being cold and calculating, until she got angry as the defence cross-examined her. Then she let slip details of her involvement in the murders, which irretrievably damaged her case. The defence also highlighted inconsistencies in Fred West's confessions and suggested he lied to protect his wife. There might not have been any direct evidence against Rosemary West, but the circumstantial evidence proved to be enough for the jury. They found her guilty on all ten counts of murder. The judge sentenced her to life imprisonment, saying 'If attention is paid to what I think, you will never be released.' The minimum term

was set at 25 years, meaning Rosemary West will not be eligible for release before 2019. A year after the trial finished the house in Cromwell Street was demolished and the bricks ground up and disposed of in a landfill site.

The police continued to investigate the activities of Fred and Rosemary West. They could not establish the whereabouts of nine more young women who had lived at Cromwell Street over the years. It is difficult to believe that the couple only killed one person, their daughter Heather, in the fifteen years between the murder of Alison Chambers in 1979 and their arrest in 1994. Persistent rumours of another burial ground, as yet undiscovered, containing many more bodies remain. Before he committed suicide, Fred West told Janet Leach there were 20 more victims whose bodies had not been found. He said he would reveal the location of one of them every year, but died before elaborating any further. Fred West was a compulsive liar, so it is hard to know if there was any truth in what he said. If Rosemary West knows anything about any other victims, she has, so far, kept it to herself.

MURDERS
5

METHOD
TORTURE
STARVATION

EXECUTION
LIFE
IMPRISONMENT

MARC
DUTROUX

# Was Marc Dutroux the **kingpin** behind a number of **kidnappings, rapes** and **murders** in Belgium from the mid '80s to the mid '90s? Or, as he claimed at his trial, **was he simply the scapegoat** for a number of the country's **top officials** and politicians keen to **cover up** their involvement in a **murderous paedophile ring?**

In comparison to many other serial killers, Marc Dutroux was not prolific, but the horrific nature of his crimes against young girls has made him the most reviled man in Belgian history. Up until his arrest in 1996, he, along with a number of accomplices, committed a series of kidnappings, rapes and murders of girls between the ages of 8 and 19. When the horrendous nature of the crimes first came to light it shattered the perception held by many Belgium people of the country being relatively safe. Almost every aspect of the case, from the botched investigation to the endless delays of the trial, has been hugely controversial. From the time of his arrest onwards, Dutroux has claimed he was just one of many people involved in a child pornography and prostitution ring, which, according to him, involved many prominent Belgian men, including politicians and top-ranking policemen. Although no evidence of the existence of such an organization has ever been uncovered, many people in Belgium are convinced there must be some truth to the allegations.

Marc Dutroux had a long history of criminal activity. He was involved in selling stolen cars in Eastern Europe, drug trafficking and had been arrested for numerous other offences. Although registered as unemployed, he owned a number of houses in different parts of Belgium. Most of them remained empty and were used by Dutroux for his illegal activities. In February 1986 he was arrested, along with his partner Michelle Martin, and charged with the rape of five young girls. It took more than three years for the case to go through the courts until, eventually, they were found guilty. Dutroux was sentenced to 13 years in prison and Martin to 5 years as

ABOVE: The secret cellar at the house of Belgian serial killer Marc Dutroux.

his accomplice. As a result of the lenient treatment of sex offenders in Belgium at that time, together with his record of good behaviour, Dutroux was released on parole in April 1992 after serving only three years of the sentence. At the time of his release, Dutroux's mother wrote to the prison governor saying she thought he would go straight back to crime.

After his release he was given a disability pension and prescribed sleeping pills and sedatives, drugs he would use to keep the girls he kidnapped quiet. He built a dungeon in the basement of a house he owned in Charleroi, in southern Belgium. It had soundproofed walls and a concrete door, which was concealed behind shelving. It is not known exactly when he first began to use the dungeon. Between 1992 and 1995 the police were informed a number of times about him, including by his mother, but took no action. Dutroux even approached a police informant and offered him money to abduct young girls. Dutroux told the informant about the dungeon in his house and said he was using it to hold girls so he could make pornographic videos of them.

On 24 June 1995, Dutroux kidnapped two eight-year-old girls, Julie Lejuene and Melissa Russo, and held them in the dungeon. Later that year he was investigated for car theft and the police

## DUTROUX HAD DRUGGED WEINSTEIN AND BURIED HIM ALIVE

searched his house on two occasions without finding the dungeon or the girls, who were still alive at that point. He was held in custody between December 1995 and March 1996 for the car thefts and, during this time, the two girls starved to death. On his release he buried them in the back yard. After their bodies were found, he told police he had killed an accomplice, Bernard Weinstein, because he had not fed the girls while Dutroux was in custody. The body was found buried next to them. Dutroux had drugged Weinstein and buried him alive.

In August 1995, while the two little girls were being held in the dungeon, Dutroux and another accomplice, Michel Lelievre, abducted An Marcaal and Eefje Lembreks. They were held at another of the houses owned by Dutroux for several weeks, before being killed and buried in concrete under a shed in the garden.

Dutroux and Lelievre kidnapped Sabine Dardenne in May 1996 and Laetitia Delhez, in August. Both were held in the dungeon and repeatedly raped while being filmed. A witness had seen a car driving slowly around the neighbourhood just before Laetitia Delhez disappeared and remembered enough of the licence plates for the police to match it to Dutroux's car. Dutroux, Michelle Martin and Michel Lelievre were all arrested. Nothing was found when the police searched the house, but, after two days in custody, Dutroux told the police where the two girls were and they were both found alive. Both would later give evidence against Dutroux at his trial.

It took more than seven years for the trial to begin. During that period Dutroux escaped by overpowering a prison guard and stealing his gun, but he was recaptured after three hours of freedom. One of the investigating judges was controversially removed from the case after attending a fundraising party held by the families of the victims. The Belgium public thought his removal had more to do with his investigation into the links between Dutroux and the alleged child pornography network. Dissatisfaction with the slow speed of the proceedings against Dutroux and the inept way the police had dealt with the case led to the largest peacetime demonstration in the history of the country. More than 300,000 people marched in Brussels. The Belgium government was forced into action. The police force was completely reorganized and a number of prominent politicians sacked.

The trial began on 1 March 2004. Dutroux tried to blame his accomplices and said he was a small part of a much larger organization, without providing details of it. The jury found him guilty on all charges and he was sentenced to life imprisonment. Michel Lelievre was sentenced to 25 years in prison and Michelle Martin to 30 years. A fourth man, Jean-Michel Nihoul, who Dutroux claimed was the brains behind the network, was acquitted of kidnapping and murder, but sentenced to 5 years on separate drug-related charges.

BELOW: The coffins containing the remains of Melissa Russo and Julie Lejeune are carried into Liege's Saint Martin Basilica during their funerals, 22 August 1996.

MURDERS
200+

METHOD
LETHAL
INJECTION

SENTENCE
LIFE
IMPRISONMENT

OUTCOME
SUICIDE

HAROLD
SHIPMAN

**Harold Shipman preyed on elderly female patients – the very people he had promised to protect and heal. A doctor who nurtured an unhealthy fascination with the effects of diamorphine – he saw himself as a god-like figure whose medical knowledge afforded him power over life and death.**

On 24 June 1998 Dr Harold Shipman signed the death certificate of 81-year-old Kathleen Grundy, one of the patients of his medical practice in Hyde, Cheshire. It was something he had done on numerous occasions in the past, an unpleasant but necessary part of any doctor's job. Her death came as an enormous shock to her family. Considering her age, she had appeared to be in perfect health. Dr Shipman visited her a few hours before she died and was the last person to see her alive. The visit had nothing to do with any health worries. He asked if he could collect a blood sample from the old lady for a study he said he was conducting into the health of his elderly patients. At the time there were no suspicious circumstances to her death. She was an elderly woman and, on her death certificate, Shipman gave the cause of death simply as old age.

A few weeks later, Kathleen Grundy's will was read out to, among others, Angela Woodruff, her daughter. The main beneficiary, receiving all of Mrs Grundy's money, and her house, was Harold Shipman. Woodruff's suspicions were aroused. Her mother had never mentioned leaving anything at all to Shipman in her will. She contacted the police and an investigation began. The typewriter used to draw up the will was found to be one owned by Shipman.

It was not the first time questions about Shipman's conduct had been asked. A few months previously Dr

ABOVE: Hilda Hibbert, one of Harold Shipman's many elderly female victims.

them were fully clothed and either sitting in a chair on lying on a sofa. In his experience, people died in a wide variety of situations. The similarities between the circumstances of the deaths of so many of Shipman's elderly female patients struck him as strange. Dr Booth, already worried about the high death rate of his patients, was now convinced something was wrong. She was not sure if it was due to incompetence or if there was something more sinister going on, so she decided to take her concerns to the local coroner. A police investigation began, but the officers assigned to the case found no evidence of malpractice. They couldn't have looked very hard.

The discovery of the forged will in June caused the police to begin a much more serious investigation. They obtained a court order to exhume Kathleen Grundy's body, and an examination revealed traces of diamorphine in her body. There was no medical reason why Mrs Grundy should have been taking diamorphine – an extremely powerful painkiller analogous with heroin. It would normally only be prescribed in very serious cases, such as during the treatment of terminally ill cancer patients.

Susan Booth, who worked for a different medical practice in Hyde, had raised concerns about him. Over the past few years he had asked her to countersign an unusually high number of cremation certificates, which are required under British law before a cremation can take place. A funeral director told her that, when he went to pick up the bodies of elderly women after Shipman signed a death certificate, he found many of

Shipman was arrested on 7 September 1998. It became apparent very quickly that he had killed many of the patients in his care with overdoses of diamorphine,

# THE SIMILARITIES BETWEEN THE CIRCUMSTANCES OF SO MANY OF SHIPMAN'S ELDERLY FEMALE PATIENTS STRUCK HIM AS STRANGE

then forged their medical records to make it look like they had been sufficiently ill to warrant the treatment. It was not a question of whether or not Shipman murdered some of his patients. The question was, how many of them did he kill? Some undoubtedly died of natural causes and some of the bodies were cremated, making it impossible to say for sure how they died. Exhuming all the bodies of those who were buried was a daunting prospect. Potentially there were hundreds of cases.

On 5 October 1999 Shipman was put on trial for the murder of 15 elderly women who died between 1995 and 1998 while in his care, including Kathleen Grundy. The police described the case of Kathleen Grundy as a sample, which would be tried first so the jury didn't become overburdened by the extent of the evidence being presented to them.

It was thought there could be in excess of 200 more cases to follow. The trial lasted for four months and, in January 2000, the jury found Shipman guilty of all 15 murders. He was sentenced to 15 consecutive life sentences, with a recommendation from the judge that he never be released. Four years later, on 13 January 2004, with the investigation into his other victims continuing, Shipman committed suicide in his prison cell by hanging himself from the bars of his window using torn up bed sheets. At no stage between his arrest and suicide did Shipman offer any form of explanation for the murders. David Blunkett, the Home Secretary at the time, famously said that, on hearing the news of the suicide when he woke in the morning, he wondered if it was too early in the day to open a bottle of champagne.

BELOW: The scene at Hyde Cemetery in Manchester as police dig in the eighth exhumation of Dr Harold Shipman's murder victims.

**THE SHIPMAN INQUIRY**

Chairman: Dame Janet Smith DBE

ABOVE: High Court judge Dame Janet Smith concludes that Shipman murdered at last 215 of his elderly patients during the Shipman Inquiry in July 2002.

OPPOSITE PAGE: Funeral directors leave Wakefield prison where Dr Harold Shipman committed suicide on 13 January 2004.

It is impossible to say for sure what motivated Shipman to kill so many of his patients. Many commentators point to the relationship he had with his mother – one of the obvious starting points in the consideration of any serial killer. Vera Shipman was probably the only person in Shipman's life to unconditionally believe in his abilities, with the possible exception of his wife who continues to protest his innocence. When Shipman was growing up, his mother constantly told him he was a bit better than everybody else, instilling a sense of superiority in him that he would carry throughout his life. Many of the people who worked with Shipman during his medical career found him aloof and

arrogant, although he is said to have had an extremely good bedside manner, particularly with elderly women.

In 1963, when Shipman was seventeen, his mother developed lung cancer. He spent many hours sitting by her bedside. As the disease progressed, her doctor gradually increased the dosage of diamorphine he prescribed to her for the pain, up until she died in June of that year. It is always easy to speculate in hindsight, but, perhaps it was during this traumatic period that Shipman developed a fascination with drugs – how they can be used to control pain and, in certain circumstances, to control life and death. It was also when he decided to pursue a career in the medical profession. Shipman's sense of superiority, together with a wish to control other people's lives and, ultimately, their deaths, would prove to be a fatal combination. After he became a general practitioner, he over-prescribed diamorphine to those patients who actually needed it, hoarded the excess and, when he decided one of his patients had lived for long enough, killed them with an overdose.

It is not known for certain exactly when he first began to kill his patients. He could have been using overdoses of prescription drugs to kill people throughout his career, beginning in Pontefract General Infirmary, West Yorkshire, in 1968. Shipman stayed there for six years, before, in 1974, becoming a general practitioner in Todmorden, a small town in the Calder Valley of West Yorkshire. While there he quickly gained a reputation as a hard worker. The other doctors in the practice particularly appreciated his willingness to take on elderly female patients, who, they often found, were the most difficult and unrewarding patients to deal with. Shipman was very popular with his elderly patients. He was not as impatient as some of the other doctors, taking the time to sit by their beds and talk to them.

In July 1975 Shipman was found to be writing prescriptions for large quantities of pethidine, a powerful painkiller sometimes known by the brand name Demerol. He was injecting it himself and had become addicted. After voluntarily entering a drug rehabilitation clinic, and pleading guilty to charges of forging prescriptions, he was given a second chance by the British Medical Council. Rather than strike his name from the register of doctors, which would have meant he would never have been able to practice as a doctor again, he was fined and warned about his future conduct.

After coming out of the clinic, Shipman worked for 18 months for the local heath authority in Durham. In 1977 he went back into general practice at the Donnybrook Medical Centre in Hyde. Although not particularly popular with other members of staff, who found him arrogant and bad-tempered, once again he took on many of the elderly female patients. In 1993 he split from the Donnybrook practice, setting himself up in a clinic on his own a few hundred yards away. Many of his elderly female patients followed him to the new practice. It would later become apparent that, during the five years he worked on his own up until his arrest in 1998, the death rate among his elderly patients rapidly increased.

The Shipman Inquiry, headed by Dame Janet Smith, was set up after Shipman was convicted in 2000. It led to the publication of a number of reports into how Shipman had got away with murder for so long. The last of the reports, which came out in 2005, made recommendations to the British Medical Council concerning changes to the procedures followed by doctors in the event of the death of a patient. It was an attempt to make sure that no doctor would ever have the opportunity to repeat the crimes committed by Shipman. The report also contained an estimate of the likely number of Shipman's victims, based on how many patients could be expected to die of natural causes during a doctor's career. Over his whole career, 459 patients died while in Shipman's care, leading to the report estimating he murdered at least 250 people. It will probably never be known for certain how many people Shipman murdered in total, but, if the figure of 250 is accepted, then Harold Shipman, a doctor entrusted with the care of the sick, becomes the most prolific serial killer in history.

MURDERS
6

METHOD
SHOOTING

A.K.A.
SON OF
SAM

DAVID
BERKOWITZ

The Son of Sam prowled the streets of the Bronx and Queens hunting for 'fair game - tasty meat' as he himself put it in a letter to the NYPD. Was David Berkowitz driven mad by the barking of his neighbour's black Labrador, or was he involved in the operations of a satanic cult who were killing as a collective?

The first of the shootings in the New York boroughs of the Bronx and Queens which would become known as the Son of Sam killings, occurred at about 1am on the night of 29 July 1976. Donna Lauria, eighteen, was sitting in the passenger seat of nineteen-year-old Jody Valenti's car, parked in front of the apartment building in the Bronx where she lived with her parents. A man approached the passenger side door and pulled a large calibre handgun out of a paper bag he was carrying. As Donna Lauria opened the car door to get out, he crouched into a firing position and shot five times into the car. He hit Lauria in the neck, killing her instantly. Jody Valenti was hit in the thigh and slumped forward onto the steering wheel, sounding the horn. The man continued to pull the trigger, even though he had already emptied the chamber of bullets, and then ran off.

Jody Valenti survived and described the shooter as being a white male, about thirty years old with black curly hair. The police recovered one of the bullets and found it was from a .44 Bulldog gun, an unusual weapon which was very powerful, but only accurate at close range. At first they thought there might be a Mafia connection to the killing because both girls were of Italian heritage. But even the Mafia didn't go around shooting teenage girls. It looked much more like a random act of madness.

Late at night on 23 October, the shooter struck again in Queens. He emptied the chamber of his .44 Bulldog into a parked car in which Carl Denaro, twenty, and Rosemary Keenan, eighteen, were sitting. Denaro was shot in the back of the head, but, although seriously injured, survived. Rosemary Keenan, the daughter of a New York Police Department detective who would later take part in the investigation, was unhurt. On 27 November, at around midnight, eighteen-year-old Joanne Lomino and her friend Donna DeMasi, sixteen, got off a bus in Queens and began to walk home from the bus stop. They noticed a man near the apartment block where Joanne Lomino lived. He asked them for directions, but, before they could answer, pulled a gun and

fired several times. Lomino was hit in the back. The bullet severed her spine, leaving her permanently paralysed. Another bullet hit Donna DeMasi, breaking her collarbone and narrowly missing a major artery, but she would go on to make a full recovery. Both young women described the attacker as having shoulder-length blond hair. The description was corroborated by a witness who saw a blond-haired man with a gun in his hand running from the scene. At this stage none of the attacks had been connected. One had been in the Bronx and the descriptions of the man involved in the two attacks in Queens were different.

The fourth shooting was also in Queens. On 29 January 1977 Christine Freund was with her boyfriend, John Diel in his car. It was late at night and cold. The car windows were misted up and they didn't see the gunman approaching. He fired three times into the car through the passenger window, hitting Freund. She died four hours later in hospital. Diel was unhurt, but didn't get a good look at the shooter. Bullets recovered from the scene matched those that had killed Donna Lauria, but it would still be some time before all the shootings were found to be connected.

On 8 March 1977, Virginia Voskerichian a young student from a family who had emigrated to America from Bulgaria, was shot once in the face at close range while she was walking home from college. She was killed instantly. The bullet was from a .44 Bulldog and matched the other bullets recovered from the previous scenes of shootings. The police couldn't find any connection between the victims or establish if they

BELOW: A note penned by the Son of Sam killer David Berkowitz.
OPPOSITE PAGE: New York mayor Abraham Beame looks on as detective Edward Zigo holds up a .44 caliber revolver, the alleged murder weapon of the 'Son of Sam' serial killer.

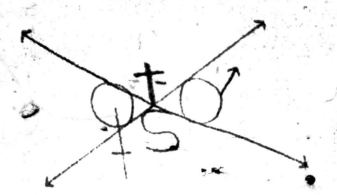

BECAUSE CRAIG IS CRAIG
SO MUST THE STREETS
BE FILLED WITH CRAIG (DEATH)

AND HUGE-DROPS OF LEAD
POURED DOWN UPON HER HEAD
UNTIL SHE WAS DEAD.
YET, THE CATS STILL COME OUT
AT NIGHT TO MATE
AND THE SPARROWS STILL
SING IN THE MORNING.

knew anybody in common. It was now obvious that a madman was randomly targeting young men and women who were out late at night in the Bronx and Queens. A task force, called Operation Omega, was set up and an announcement about the connections between the attacks made to the press. The New York newspapers came up with a name for the perpetrator – the .44 Calibre Killer.

The shooter moved back to the Bronx for his next attack. He shot and killed Alexander Esau, twenty, and Valentina Suriani, eighteen, on 17 April. They were sitting in their car late at night not far from the scene of the first attack. Esau was shot in the side of the head once and died later in hospital. Suriani, who was in the passenger seat, was hit twice in the head and died at the scene. The killer left a note in the street by the car. It was hand written in capitals and was full of spelling mistakes. It was addressed to Captain Joseph Borrelli, one of the Operation Omega detectives, and read:

I am deeply hurt by your calling me a wemon hater. I am not. But I am a monster. I am the "Son of Sam." I am a little brat. When father Sam gets drunk he gets mean. He beats his family. Sometimes he ties me up to the back of the house. Other times he locks me in the garage. Sam loves to drink blood. "Go out and kill," commands father Sam. Behind our house some rest. Mostly young – raped and slaughtered – their blood drained – just bones now. Papa Sam keeps me locked in the attic too. I can't get out but I look out the attic window and watch the world go by. I feel like an outsider. I am on a different wavelength then everybody else – programmed too kill. However, to stop me you must kill me. Attention all police: Shoot me first – shoot to kill or else keep out of my way or you will die! Papa Sam is old now. He needs some blood to preserve his youth. He has had too many heart attacks. "Ugh, me hoot, it hurts, sonny boy." I miss my pretty princess most of all. She's resting in our ladies house. But I'll see her soon. I am the "Monster" – Beelzebub – the chubby behemouth. I love to hunt. Prowling the streets looking for fair game – tasty meat. The wemon of Queens are prettyist of all. It must be the water they drink. I live for the hunt – my life. Blood for papa. Mr. Borrelli, sir, I don't want to kill anymore. No sur, no more but I must, 'honour thy father.' I want to make love to the world. I love people. I don't belong on earth. Return me to yahoos. To the people of Queens, I love you. And I want to wish all of you a happy Easter. May

God bless you in this life and in the next. And for now I say goodbye and goodnight. Police: let me haunt you with these words: I'll be back! I'll be back! To be interpreted as – bang, bang, bang, bang, bang – ugh!! Yours in murder, Mr. Monster.

It was both deranged and disturbing, and the killer said he intended to continue shooting people. From then on he became known as the Son of Sam.

A month later a letter signed Son of Sam and in similar handwriting arrived at the offices of the New York Daily News. It contained more references to Satanism and included a list of names the writer said would help the investigation, including the Duke of Death, the Twenty Two Disciples of Hell and John 'Wheaties'. He also promised to buy everyone involved in the investigation a new pair of shoes after he was caught.

On 26 June Son of Sam struck again in Queens. He shot another young couple as they sat in their car. Neither of them were killed, but they could not give a description of their attacker. A month later, on 31 July, he attacked yet another couple in a parked car, this time in South Brooklyn. Stacy Moskowitz was killed and Robert Violante, the young man she was with, was blinded. Another young couple in a car parked nearby witnessed the shooting. They described a stocky man with fair hair crouching down and shooting four times into the car before walking away. A few days later another witness, Cecelia Davis, came forward. She had seen a dark-haired man walking away from the parked cars. He took a parking ticket off the windscreen of a yellow Ford Galaxy, which was parked beside a fire hydrant, got in it and drove away. The reason she didn't come forward straight away was because the man had seen her watching him and she was terrified.

It took a week to trace the parking ticket to David Berkowitz, who worked for the US Mail and lived in Yonkers. At the time he was being investigated

BELOW: Four victims of the Son of Sam: Valentina Suriami, Christine Freund, Virginia Voskerichian and Stacey Moskovitch.
OPPOSITE PAGE: Son of Sam Killer David Berkowitz following his arrest.

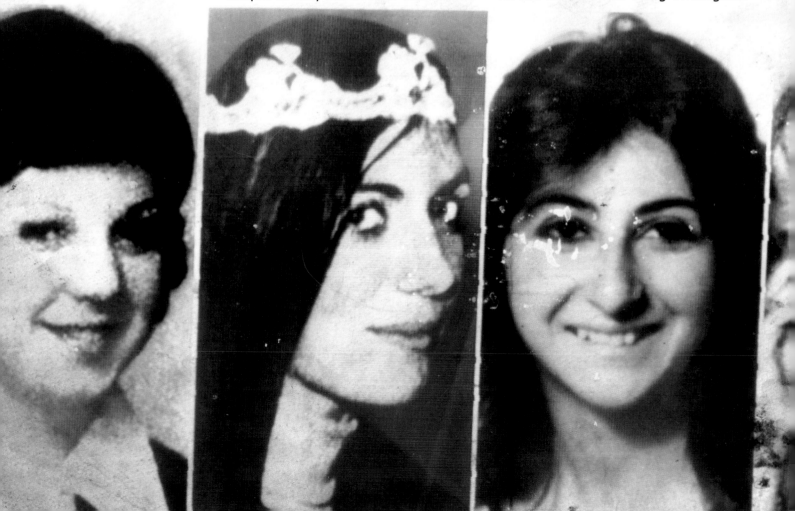

over an incident involving a series of threatening letters which had been received by one of his neighbours, Sam Carr. The letters demanded that Carr stop his black Labrador from barking all the time. Shortly afterwards the Labrador was shot and wounded with a .22 rifle.

Detectives found the yellow Galaxy parked outside Berkowitz's apartment block. Inside was a .22 rifle along with other guns and a letter addressed to Inspector Timothy Dowd, the head of Operation Omega. It was in the same handwriting as the previous Son of Sam letters and said the next killing would be on Long Island. The detectives waited for Berkowitz to come out of the apartment block and asked him his name. He said 'I am Sam' and wanted to know why it had taken the police so long to catch him.

Berkowitz gave a detailed confession to the police. He claimed he was ordered to kill people by Sam Carr and that the orders were conveyed to him by the demon voice of Carr's black Labrador. If it was an attempt to try and convince the police and the jury at his subsequent trial that he was insane, it didn't work. At the trial he was found guilty of six murders and eight attempted murders and sentenced to six life sentences, totalling 365 years in prison.

Not everybody, including some of the police who worked on the investigation, was satisfied that Berkowitz acted alone. An investigative journalist, Maury Terry, has connected Berkowitz to Sam Carr's two sons, one of whom was sometimes known as John Wheaties. Maury considers all three were involved with a Satanist cult which committed a number of other crimes, including murder, in New York, North Dakota and Los Angeles as well as the Son of Sam attacks. Both Carr brothers died within two years of Berkowitz's arrest and, although the case remains open, no further charges in connection with the killings have ever been made.

VICTIMS
**12**

A.K.A
**BELTWAY
SNIPERS**

**JOHN ALLEN
MUHAMMAD
& LEE BOYD
MALVO**

**The Beltway Snipers were renegade members of the Nation of Islam, who attempted to use the murder of innocent people to scare the US government into funding the training of a terrorist army within its own borders. It was an integrally flawed plan from the beginning but that didn't stop the death toll rising.**

At 5.20pm on 2 October 2002, a rifle bullet smashed through the window of the Aspen Hill branch of Michael's Craft Store in Montgomery County, Maryland. Nobody was hurt and, initially at least, the shooting was considered to be the act of an idiot who had got hold of a rifle. It was only later that the location, a few miles off Interstate 95 where it joins the Capital Beltway north of Washington DC, would become significant. It was the first in a series of 14 shootings occurring over the next three weeks at locations around the Capital Beltway and Interstate 95.

About 45 minutes after the first shooting, 55-year-old James Martin was shot dead outside the Shoppers Food Warehouse in Wheaton, Montgomery County, by a bullet from a high-powered rifle. It was an apparently motiveless murder, but it was only a taster of what was to come. The following day all hell broke loose in Montgomery County.

It started at 7.41am in Rockville. James Buchanan, a 39-year-old landscape gardener, was killed by a single shot from a rifle as he was mowing the grass outside the Fitzgerald Auto Mall. This was followed by two shootings in Aspen Hill within minutes of each other. Premkumar Walekar, 54, was shot dead on the forecourt of a gas station as he filled his taxi at 8.12am. Twenty-five minutes later Sarah Ramos, 34, was killed outside the Leisure World Shopping Center. Then, at 9.58am, 25-year-old Lori Lewis-Rivera was shot at a gas station in Kensington, Montgomery County. The fifth and last killing of the day came at 9.15pm. Pascal Charlot, 72, was shot while walking along Georgia Avenue, one of the main arterial roads running from Montgomery County into Washington.

All the victims were shot with a Buckmaster XM-15 semiautomatic rifle from ranges of between 50 and 100 yards. There was no obvious pattern to the shooter's choice of victim. They were of different ages and sexes and from different racial backgrounds. The police had very little information from witnesses. Nobody, it seemed, had seen the murderer.

The following day, 4 October, a 43-year-old woman was injured by a bullet from a rifle outside another branch of Michael's Craft Store in Spotsylvania County, Virginia, off Interstate 95 south of Washington. On 7 October a schoolboy was shot as he got off a bus outside his school in Bowie, Maryland. By this time the police had connected all the shootings around Washington. It looked as if the shooter was driving round the Capital Beltway, getting off at various junctions and looking for an opportunity to kill someone. It appeared that anyone who happened to come into the gunman's sights would be a target. The media found a name for what they assumed was a single killer – the Beltway Sniper.

The investigation was headed by Charles Moose, the Chief of Police in Montgomery County, and would soon involve the FBI. Moose would become a familiar figure on TV over the next few weeks as the shootings continued and media interest from

around the world intensified. By this time the attacks had been connected to two murders committed during robberies in Clinton, Maryland and Montgomery, Alabama.

On 9 October Dean Meyers, 53, was killed outside a gas station near Manassas, Maryland, and two days later Kenneth Bridges, also 53, was shot dead in similar circumstances off Interstate 95 near Fredericksburg, Virginia. There were still no witnesses who had actually seen the gunman. A white box van was seen near the scene of some of the murders and, for some time, the investigation focused on finding it. Linda Franklin, a 47-year-old FBI employee, was shot in a parking lot outside Falls Church, Virginia, on 14 October. The next victim was Jeffrey Hopper who also died in a parking lot in Ashland, Virginia, 145 km (90 miles) south of Washington. At the scene the police found a letter demanding a ransom of $100 million or the sniper would start to target children. The note also implied there were two men involved in the shootings.

Although details of the investigation were being withheld from the media, the FBI had connected the robbery in Alabama to John Allen Muhammad, a 41-

LIVE     WJZ

**BREAKING NEWS**

CNN ▶ SUSPECTS' VEHICLE HAS BEEN TOWED TO MONTGOMERY CO    S&P

year-old veteran of the first Gulf War. He had changed his name from Williams to Muhammad in 2001 after joining the Nation of Islam and had an ex-wife who lived near the Capital Beltway. A dark-blue Chevrolet Caprice was registered in his name and had been seen near some of the murder scenes. The police were looking for a white van at the time and had taken no notice of it.

On 22 October Conrad Johnson was shot as he got off the bus he was driving in Aspen Hill. The police appealed to the public for information on the Chevrolet Caprice. Reports came in on 24 October of two men sleeping in a dark-blue Caprice at a rest stop off Interstate 70 near Myersville, Maryland. Armed police and FBI agents surrounded the car and John Allen Muhammad and seventeen-year-old Lee Boyd Malvo were arrested. The car had been modified with a firing point for a rifle in the trunk. Muhammad, the shooter, could crawl into the trunk without getting out of the car. It was the end of a three-week killing spree which

left ten people dead and three seriously wounded.

At their trial in Virginia in 2003, John Allen Muhammad was sentenced to death and Lee Boyd Malvo, who was too young to face the death penalty, was given life imprisonment. Both were then extradited to Maryland to stand trial where the majority of the murders had occurred. In May 2006 Malvo gave the first detailed account of the plans Muhammad had developed. The shootings around Washington were only the first phase. Initially they were going to shoot six people a day for a month, which proved impossible, then move on to Baltimore. The ultimate goal was to extort millions of dollars from the US government to finance the recruitment and training of a small army of terrorists, who would be unleashed in a wave of coordinated attacks across America. After the trial, at which both men were found guilty of the six murders committed in Maryland, they were sent back to prisons in Virginia where they remain.

OPPOSITE PAGE: Television image courtesy of WJZ via CNN shows Maryland police manoeuvring the vehicle used by the sniper suspects John Allen Muhammad and his stepson John Lee Malvo. ABOVE: ATF agent Walter A. Dandridge Jr. holds the bushmaster rifle used by the snipers, during his testimony in the trial of John Allen Muhammad.

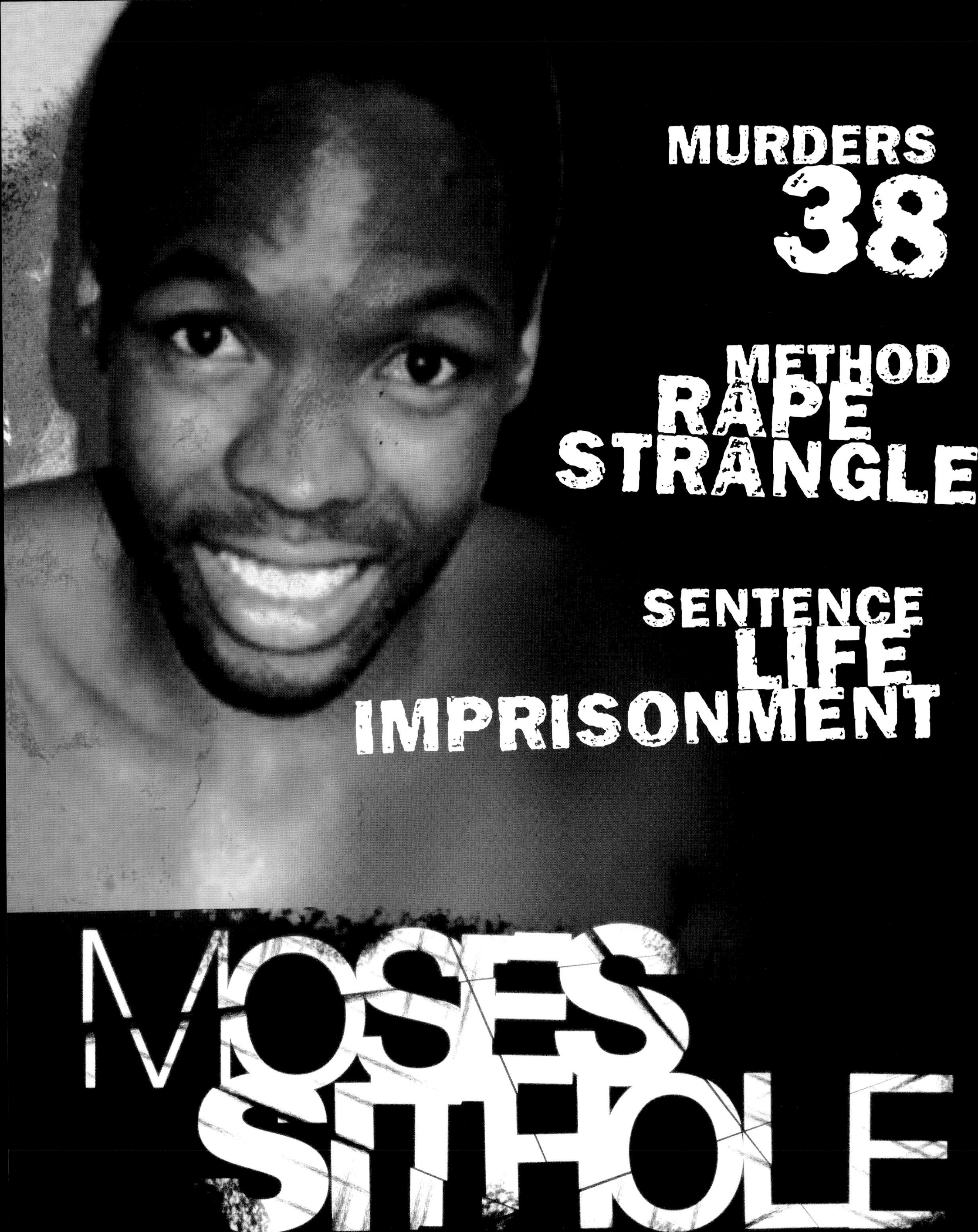

MURDERS
**38**

METHOD
**RAPE STRANGLE**

SENTENCE
**LIFE IMPRISONMENT**

MOSES SITHOLE

**Moses Sithole used the promise of employment to lure women into secluded areas before raping and strangling them. At his trial he claimed his actions were revenge for six years of false imprisonment, but nothing could justify taking their lives.**

Since the end of the apartheid era in South Africa in 1994, one of the major social problems faced by the country has been the soaring levels of violent crime. It has the second highest per capita levels of rape and murder in the world, after the USA, and has faced an epidemic of serial killing. Some of the townships, created under apartheid to segregate the black population, have been particularly badly affected. Of all the South African serial killers, Moses Sithole stands out, becoming notorious because of the number of young women he raped and killed. Multiple victims were found first in Atteridgeville, a township west of Pretoria, and then in Boksburg, 64 km (40 miles) to the south. His name was also linked to another series of killings in Cleveland, a suburb of Johannesburg, leading to the news media dubbing him the ABC Murderer.

The first body was found in a field in Atteridgeville on 4 January 1995. It was badly decomposed and could not be identified. The woman had been strangled and, as her clothing was in disarray, the police concluded she had also been raped. On 9 February the naked body of 27-year-old Beauty Soko, who had gone missing in Atteridgeville in January, was found. She had also been raped and strangled. Her clothes had then been piled on top of her body and weighted down with stones. The third victim was found on 6 March, partially buried in a ditch. It was Sara Mokono, 25, who had disappeared three days earlier. A month later Letta Ndlangamandla, also 25, was discovered. Her hands were tied behind her back with her bra before she was raped and strangled. The body of her two-year-old son was found the following day. He had been hit on the head, but a pathologist could not say for sure if the blow killed him or if he had died from exposure.

Over the next three months five more bodies of young women were found around Atteridgeville, all killed in the same way. A police task force was set up and Micki Pistorius, a psychological profiler, was brought in. She thought the killer was in his late twenties and was capable of talking the women he attacked into going with him to the locations where they were killed. The next attack occurred near Boksburg. A witness, Absalom Sangweni, saw a couple walking on the veld in the distance, but the man returned later on his own. Sangweni went to see what had happened and found the body of 25-year-old Josephine Mlangeni. She had left home that morning to meet a man about a potential job offer.

More attacks followed. Bodies were now being found in several other locations around Pretoria as well as Atteridgeville and Boksburg. The intervals between the attacks was getting shorter, and the killer was refining his technique. He was tying his victim's hands and feet, presumably to give himself more control over them, and using a garrotte to kill them. On 12 September a body was found in Cleveland. It matched the other killings and was very similar to a series of eleven killings that happened there the previous year. David Selepe had been arrested and charged with those murders. Before he had been brought to trial he died in police custody, apparently during an escape attempt. Now it looked like they might have got the wrong man. Four days later another body turned up in Boksburg, at the Van Dyk Mine near Boksburg Prison. Over the next few days, nine more bodies were found in the immediate area. They had been killed over a period of several months, mostly where they were found.

Micki Pistorius met Robert Ressler, the man who pioneered profiling for the FBI, at a conference and asked him to help. Most of the victims were women in their 20s or early 30s and were either unemployed or looking for a better job. The killer appeared to be luring women to meet him with the offer of work. Ressler thought the murderer held a grudge against one particular woman, who would be similar to the victims, and was symbolically killing her over and over again. He also thought the Cleveland murders were committed by the ABC Murderer and David Selepe together, although this has never been proven.

BELOW: Robert K Ressler, leading serial killer expert for the FBI.

One of the victims found in Boksburg was identified as Amelia Rapodile, shortly after her body was discovered. Detectives traced her movements on 7 September, the day she went missing, and found she had arranged to meet a man called Moses Sithole. He ran an organization called Youth Against Human Abuse and had offered Rapodile a job. In the meantime Tryphina Mogotsi had gone missing from Benoni, a town near Boksburg. Sithole had visited the charity where she worked a few days before she disappeared. The police were convinced he was the killer.

The publicity surrounding the murders was now at fever pitch. President Nelson Mandela appealed for residents in the townships to help the police. It was only a year since apartheid had finally come to an end, during which the townships had virtually been at war with the authorities. In October a man phoned a newspaper in Cape Town and claimed to be the killer, saying 'I am the man so highly wanted.' He said a woman had falsely accused him of rape, resulting in a six-year prison sentence, and he was taking revenge. To prove he really was the killer, he gave details of the location of the body of a missing woman. Shortly afterwards Sithole phoned his brother-in-law and told him he needed a gun. They arranged to meet, but the man phoned the police. They were waiting for Sithole when he arrived for the meeting. When challenged by a police officer, Sithole attacked him with an axe. The officer shot Sithole in the leg and stomach and he was arrested and taken to hospital.

At his trial in 1996 Sithole was charged with 38 murders, 40 rapes and 6 counts of robbery. Many of the rapes had occurred in the 1980s and four of the murder counts related to the Cleveland series attributed to David Selepe. The trial continued for more than a year. Despite the mountain of evidence linking him to the crimes and a huge number of witnesses, including his own sister, for the prosecution, Sithole continued to protest his innocence. On 4 December 1997 he was found guilty on all charges and was sentenced on each one individually. He was given 50 years for each murder, 12 years for every rape and 5 years for each robbery. It came to a staggering 2,410 years in prison. As if he needed to elaborate, the judge said 'I want to make it clear that Sithole should stay in jail for the rest of his life.'

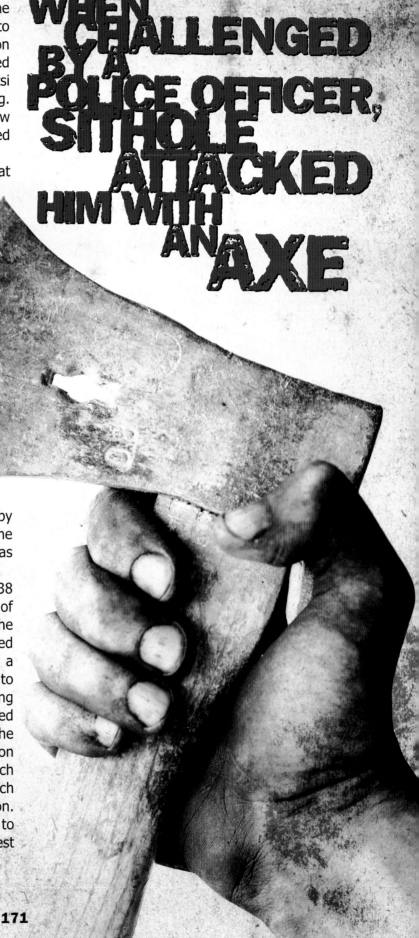

# WHEN CHALLENGED BY A POLICE OFFICER, SITHOLE ATTACKED HIM WITH AN AXE

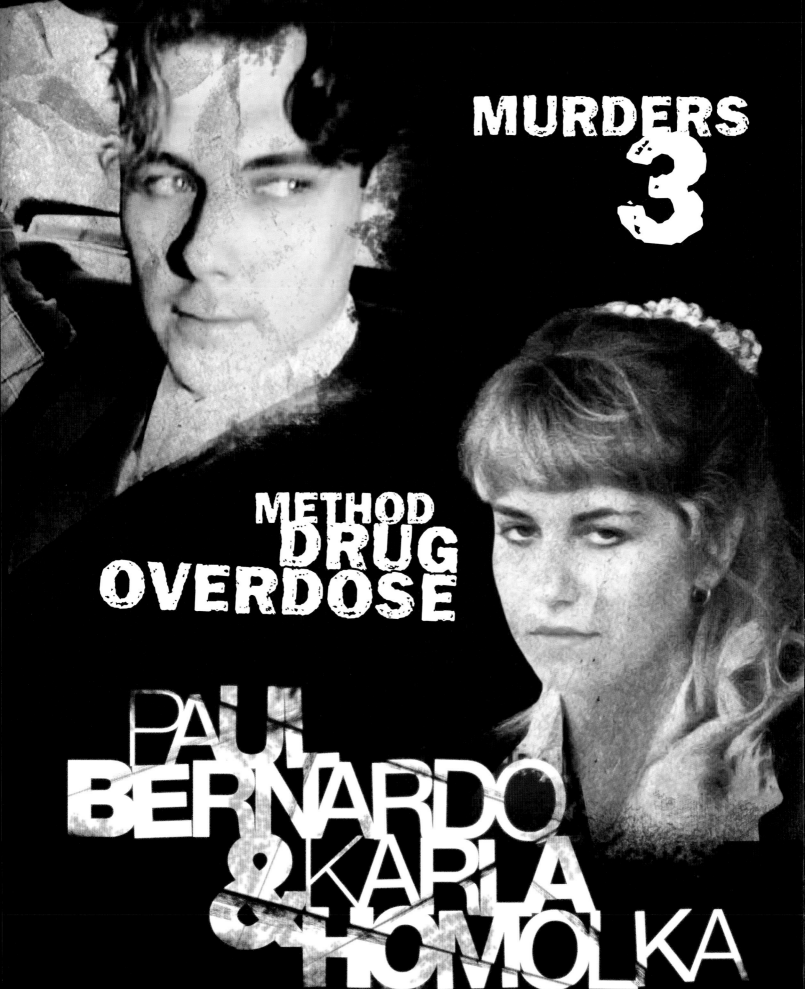

MURDERS
3

METHOD
DRUG
OVERDOSE

PAUL
BERNARDO
& KARLA
HOMOLKA

# Paul Bernardo and Karla Homolka were deeply in love. They were also deeply disturbed. On the surface they appeared to have everything going for them, but scratch that surface and it soon became clear that all was not as it seemed.

On the surface Paul Bernardo and Karla Homolka appeared to have everything going for them. They were both good looking and successful and, after meeting in 1987, fell completely in love with one another. Bernardo had just left the University of Toronto and was working as an accountant with Price Waterhouse and Homolka worked in a veterinary clinic. In 1990 they got engaged, planning to get married the following year. Beneath this veneer of respectability, a much darker picture would emerge of the relationship between what the media would call the Ken and Barbie of Murder and Mayhem. Bernardo demanded perverted and sadistic sex from Homolka and treated her as his sex slave. She complied with all his demands, encouraging him to go further and further. But there was one thing she couldn't give him. She was not a virgin when they met and he wanted to take her virginity.

In November 1990 Bernardo was interviewed by detectives investigating a series of rapes in Scarborough, the suburb of Toronto where Bernardo was from, between May 1987 and May 1990. His name came up in the investigation a number of times and he fitted the composite picture drawn up of the Scarborough Rapist, as the perpetrator was being called. The detectives took hair, saliva and blood samples from Bernardo and sent them for forensic testing and DNA profiling. It took more than two years for the results of the tests to come back.

Shortly after the police interview Bernardo persuaded Karla Homolka that, as he had not been able to take her virginity, the next best thing would be to have sex with her fifteen-year-old sister. Homolka agreed, saying she would give Tammy Lyn Homolka to Bernardo as a Christmas present. She stole Halcion, a powerful sedative, from the veterinary clinic where she worked. On the evening of 23 December 1990, while staying at Karla's parents house, they spiked Tammy Lyn's drink with the drug. The combination of alcohol and sedative knocked Tammy Lyn out quickly and, while her parents were sleeping upstairs, Bernardo viciously raped her. Karla Homolka videotaped the assault and made sure her sister didn't regain consciousness by holding a cloth soaked in halothane, an anaesthetic, over her face. After Bernardo finished, Karla Homolka also raped Tammy Lyn. At some point during her ordeal Tammy Lyn threw up and choked to death on her own vomit. Bernardo and Homolka cleaned up and, early the next morning, called an ambulance. The rest of Homolka's family thought Tammy Lyn's death was a tragic accident. They had no idea of Bernardo and Homolka's involvement.

In the New Year Bernardo and Homolka moved to a house in Port Dalhousie, near St. Catherines, on the other side of Lake Ontario from Toronto. Bernardo was involved in a cigarette smuggling operation across the American border and gave up his job at Price Waterhouse to concentrate on it. Over the next six months a series of rapes occurred around St. Catherines. The police connected them to those committed by the Scarborough Rapist, but still didn't have the results of the tests carried out on Bernardo.

Late at night on 15 June 1991 Bernardo was in Burlington, near Toronto, looking for car licence plates to steal. He wanted them to disguise his own car when he was driving across the border smuggling. That night fourteen-year-old Leslie Mahaffy got back late from a night out and her parents had accidentally locked her out. She was standing outside her house when Bernardo saw her. He abducted Mahaffy and took her back to Port Dalhousie. Once there Bernardo and Homolka repeatedly raped the young girl. The following day they killed her and cut the body up with a power saw. Then they encased the body parts in concrete and dumped the blocks in Lake Gibson, not far from St. Catherines. Two weeks later a couple out canoeing on the lake found the concrete blocks, which

**KARLA HOMOLKA VIDEOTAPED THE ASSAULT AND MADE SURE HER SISTER DIDN'T REGAIN CONSCIOUSNESS**

RIGHT: Karla Homolka arrives at court.

had been dumped where the lake was quite shallow, and called the police. On the same day Bernardo and Homolka were married in a lavish ceremony at Niagara Falls. The newly-weds went on their honeymoon to Hawaii. While they were there a number of rapes occurred, which would later be connected to the Scarborough Rapist.

The following year, on 16 April 1992, Karla Homolka approached Kirsten French, a fifteen-year-old girl, in the car park of a Catholic church and asked her for directions. Bernardo came up behind the girl with a knife and forced her into his car. They took Kirsten French back to their house where, over the course of the next two days, they viciously sexually assaulted and tortured her. They took turns to rape her while the other one operated the video camera. Kirsten French's body was found in a ditch near Burlington on 30 April. It was dumped there by Bernardo and Homolka in an attempt to confuse the police.

Paul Bernardo was arrested on 6 January 1993 after he attacked his wife with a screwdriver. He was allowed out on bail and Homolka went to live with her surviving sister. A month later, the results of the DNA test conducted on him in 1990 finally came through. His DNA matched samples found at the scene of the Scarborough rapes. Bernardo was put under 24-hour surveillance and Homolka was interviewed about the rapes. Gradually Homolka admitted to being involved. In May 1993, she was offered a plea bargain to give a full confession. In exchange for a charge of manslaughter, which carried a maximum sentence of 12 years, Homolka gave details of the murders of Leslie Mahaffy and Kirsten French. Canadian newspapers described it as a deal with the devil.

Bernardo was arrested and the videos of the assaults were recovered from his lawyer, who resigned from the case in order to be legally able to pass them to the prosecution. At first Bernardo claimed the deaths had been accidental, then he changed his story, saying Homolka had been the instigator of the murders. At his trial, Bernardo was found guilty of both murders and sentenced to life in prison. The evidence was enough to convict him without Homolka's confession. The Canadian public were scandalized, knowing that a woman who, at the very least, was an accessory to the murders of two young girls had got off so lightly.

Karla Homolka was released from prison in 2005 after serving the full term of her 12-year sentence. Paul Bernardo remains in prison. So far he has admitted to a total of 25 rapes. The police believe he has committed many more and may also have been responsible for the disappearance of a number of other young girls in Ontario before he was arrested in 1993.

MURDERS
**5**

VICTIMS
GAY
MEN

A.K.A.
THE GAY
SLAYER
/ THE FAIRY
LIQUIDATOR

# COLIN IRELAND

As police forced the door of the apartment in Battersea, London they were **confronted by two dogs** who led them to a bedroom where their **master lay naked**, sprawled across his four-poster bed. His head was covered by a **plastic bag** tied securely round his neck and his **wrists and ankles tightly bound.**

Colin Ireland dreamed of becoming a serial killer, aware that to earn this title he would have to kill a minimum of four people. Born on 16 March 1954, Ireland suffered the embarrassment of extreme poverty and the label of 'bastard' in his early years. His mother was only seventeen years old when she fell pregnant and, having been abandoned by her lover, decided to leave the father's name blank on Ireland's birth certificate. Immature and unsure of how to look after her new baby, Ireland's mother went to live with her parents in Myrtle Road, Dartford. By the time Ireland was five, his mother felt she was mature enough to look after him by herself and decided to make her own way in the world. But life was a struggle for a single mum with no work and they were forced to live in a humble camp for homeless women and children, which in many ways was little better than life in a prison.

By 1961 the young Ireland had a father-figure in his life and his future didn't appear as bleak. Ireland found school difficult, because he had moved homes so many times he had never settled into a routine or made any real friends. He recalls being subjected to verbal and occasional physical abuse due to his dishevelled appearance. To avoid being bullied, Ireland started to play truant, and as punishment he was frequently subjected to the cane. A person who has lacked power early in their life often seeks to control others when they reach adulthood, and this is exactly what happened to Colin Ireland, the boy who had always been the 'odd one out'.

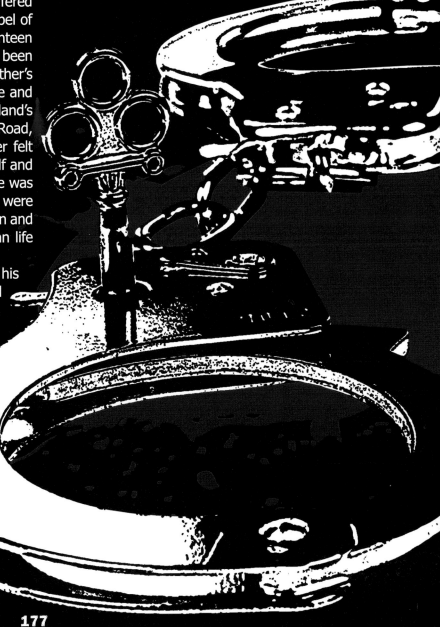

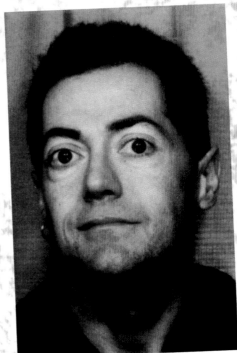

His vulnerability as a child must have been as obvious as wearing a label on his forehead because on several occasions he was approached by strange men to perform perverse acts. Always the victim, Ireland came to believe that these paedophiles had a bizarre power over other people and these experiences had a profound effect in his later life. As an adult he preyed on homosexuals, gaining notoriety as the 'Gay Slayer' or the 'Fairy Liquidator'.

Ireland did not commit his first crime until he was seventeen years old. Having been unhappy at home and at school for many years, he decided to steal some money and run away to London. However, his plans went awry when he was caught and, as part of a care order, he was sent to Finchton Manor School in Kent. Here, once again, he became the subject of ridicule. When he eventually left Finchton Ireland fulfilled his original plan and ran away to London where he quickly became a part of the 'Playland' scene. It was an area rife with paedophiles and drag queens, where boys would often sell their bodies just to get a bed for the night. Forced into a world he didn't understand and with nowhere to live and no money, it wasn't long before Ireland was once again in trouble. Although his offences were quite trivial, he was forced to spend time at Hollesly Bay, an open borstal, where he remained until he was eighteen years old.

On his release, Ireland had his first relationship with a woman, but the experience was not a happy one due his confused state of mind. He explained this time in his life as the 'lost period' often wandering about in a state of complete numbness, having neither the willpower or

# IRELAND REVELLED IN THE GOD-LIKE POWER HE WAS EXPERIENCING

LEFT: Three of Ireland's five victims, from top: Andrew Collier, Christopher Dunn and Peter Walker.

# AWARE THAT THERE WAS A SECURITY CAMERA AT THE FRONT OF THE PUB, IRELAND LED WALKER OUT USING THE SIDE DOOR

the integrity to change his way of life. By the age of 21 he was in more serious trouble with the police and spent a spell in Lewes prison, where for the first time in his life he felt secure.

Always in and out of trouble, in 1981, Ireland now aged 27, met his first wife Virginia Zammit. Virginia was nine years his senior with a five-year-old daughter, and initially they were very happy together. However, she soon tired of her husband's aggression and frequent spells of incarceration and divorced him in 1987. Two years later, Ireland met Janet Young, the landlady of The Globe in Buckfast, Devon. Ireland moved into the pub and within three months they were married but this marriage was also doomed. Within four months of being married Ireland drove his wife and her two children into town, dropped them off and then disappeared with the car and some money from the pub takings, having first cleared their joint bank account.

For a while Ireland worked at a shelter for homeless people in Essex, but he was not a very popular member of staff and was forced to resign. Ireland's frustration reached a peak and, unsure what direction to take in his life, he headed once again for London in March 1993. For some reason, something which Ireland himself couldn't explain, he found himself drawn to The Colherne, a pub on the Brompton Road in West London. It

had a reputation as being a place where homosexuals went to find a partner for the night. Ireland was wound up like a coiled spring and he felt an inexplicable urge to kill. In a way he hoped that no one would approach him, but sadly he met 45-year-old Peter Walker when he accidentally spilt his drink over Ireland's shirt. Walker urged Ireland to punish him, an invitation which he found very hard to turn down especially as he had entered the pub with his very own 'murder kit' – a knife, some rope, a pair of gloves and a change of clothes.

Aware that there was a security camera at the front of the pub, Ireland led Walker out using the side door. They walked back to Walker's flat in Battersea where he led Ireland into his bedroom after first shutting his two dogs in the kitchen out of the way. The bedroom was quite plush with a four-poster bed covered in luxurious satin sheets. Walker started to undress and told Ireland that he liked to be bound and gagged because he said he found it sexually exciting. Once Ireland had rendered his victim helpless his excitement grew into a frenzy as he suddenly realized he had total power for the first time in his life. After beating Walker with his fists, a dog lead and then a belt, he took a plastic bag and tied it securely over his head, revelling in the God-like power he was experiencing. Not quite ready to finish his perverse game, Ireland removed the bag for a couple of

# HE GRABBED SOME CONDOMS AND STUFFED SEVERAL IN WALKER'S MOUTH AND UP HIS NOSTRILS

minutes and Walker looked pathetically into his eyes and said 'I'm going to die', to which Ireland replied, 'Yes, you are'. When his victim had breathed his last, for some peculiar reason Ireland had the urge to burn Walker's pubic hair and later told the police that he was curious to see what the smell was like. When the evil deed was done, Ireland set about meticulously removing any trace that he had been present in the flat and then, worried that he might attract too much attention leaving when the roads were so quiet, decided to stay until morning. He watched television for a while but then got bored and started looking through some of Walker's personal items. He discovered to his horror that Walker was HIV-positive from some papers found in a drawer and this made him angry because he knew that Walker had intended seducing him without warning him of his condition. He was so disgusted that he grabbed some condoms and stuffed several in Walker's mouth and up his nostrils before leaving the flat. As he walked away from the scene of his first murder he wondered whether anyone could tell from the expression on his face that he had just killed someone. He returned home on a crowded commuter train, waiting for the opportunity to throw the contaminated evidence (latex gloves, change of clothes etc.) out of the window.

Two days after his first murder, Ireland made a call to the Samaritans in which he said he was concerned about Peter Walker's dogs, telling them that he had killed their owner after locking them into a room. However, his strange behaviour did not stop at one phone call, he then went on to phone *The Sun* newspaper,

telling them, 'It was my New Year's resolution to kill a homosexual. He was a homosexual and into kinky sex. You like that stuff, don't you?' The police had believed that Walker had died when a sex session had gone horribly wrong, but this was not the case if the anonymous phone caller was telling the truth.

Ireland wanted to repeat the excitement of that night but decided he would wait until the heat had died down a little before making his next move. Two months later he returned to The Colherne to seek his next victim – 37-year-old librarian Christopher Dunn. The couple went to Dunn's flat in Wealdstone where he told Ireland that he loved to be dominated. Immediately the excitement rose in his blood and Ireland told him to go and get himself ready. When Ireland walked into the bedroom, Dunn was already naked except for a body harness and a studded belt. Ireland told him to turn over and handcuffed his hands behind his head and tied his feet together. Before killing him, Ireland demanded the PIN number of Dunn's cash card so that he could later reimburse himself and restock his 'murder kit'. After beating Dunn, he held a lighter flame to his testicles and then suffocated the life out of him by placing a noose around his neck.

Only six days later, Ireland picked up a third man from the same pub. His next victim was 35-year-old Perry Bradley, a businessman and son of a US congressman. Bradley lived in Kensington in a luxurious apartment but nearly ruined Ireland's plans when he told him that he liked to be the 'dominator' when having sex. Ireland explained that he would find it impossible to get aroused if he could not be the dominant partner, and Bradley reluctantly – and foolishly – agreed. His life ended with a noose around his neck.

At first the police had not made a connection between the murders because they had all been allocated to different stations. They were struggling to find any leads as there was no evidence, no witnesses and no one had remarked upon the similarities between the three cases. It took another two murders before the police realized that there were common factors in all the deaths.

Ireland listened intently to the news on the radio and television and became angry that he had received no publicity whatsoever. He returned to the pub and picked up 33-year-old Andrew Collier, a housing warden. It was this murder that gave the police their first link because he stuffed a condom in his victim's mouth when he learned he was also HIV-positive. He also killed Collier's pet cat because he wanted to dispel any rumours that he was an animal lover, after his initial phone call to the Samaritans regarding Walker's dogs.

His fifth and final victim was 41-year-old Emanuel Spiteri, a chef from Malta. After cleaning up as normal after the event, Ireland decided to set fire to Spiteri's apartment and it would appear that after five murders his desire to murder was beginning to wane, or perhaps Ireland's lust for publicity had finally overcome his urge to kill. The following day he phoned the police to tell them to look for a body at the scene of a fire in South London. However, unbeknown to Ireland the fire had fizzled out and the body had already been reported by Spiteri's landlady.

At last the police had some clues, not only had Ireland been careless in wiping his fingerprints off the windowsill at Spiteri's apartment, he had also been spotted on a security camera at Charing Cross station. However, despite having an artist's impression of the suspected murderer the police got nowhere with their investigations. However on 21 July a burly man, over six feet tall and assessed to be in his thirties walked into a lawyer's office in Southend-on-Sea. He told the receptionist that he needed a legal representative, that his name was Colin Ireland and that he was the man the papers had branded as the 'Fairy Liquidator'.

Ireland pleaded guilty to all charges when his case came to the Old Bailey on 20 December 1993. Mr Justice Sachs suggested that he should spend the remainder of his life behind bars, adding: 'To take one human life is an outrage; to take five is carnage!' Ireland smiled as the judge read out his sentence, happy that he had achieved notoriety as a serial killer at last.

Emanuel Spiteri, the fifth victim of serial killer Colin Ireland.

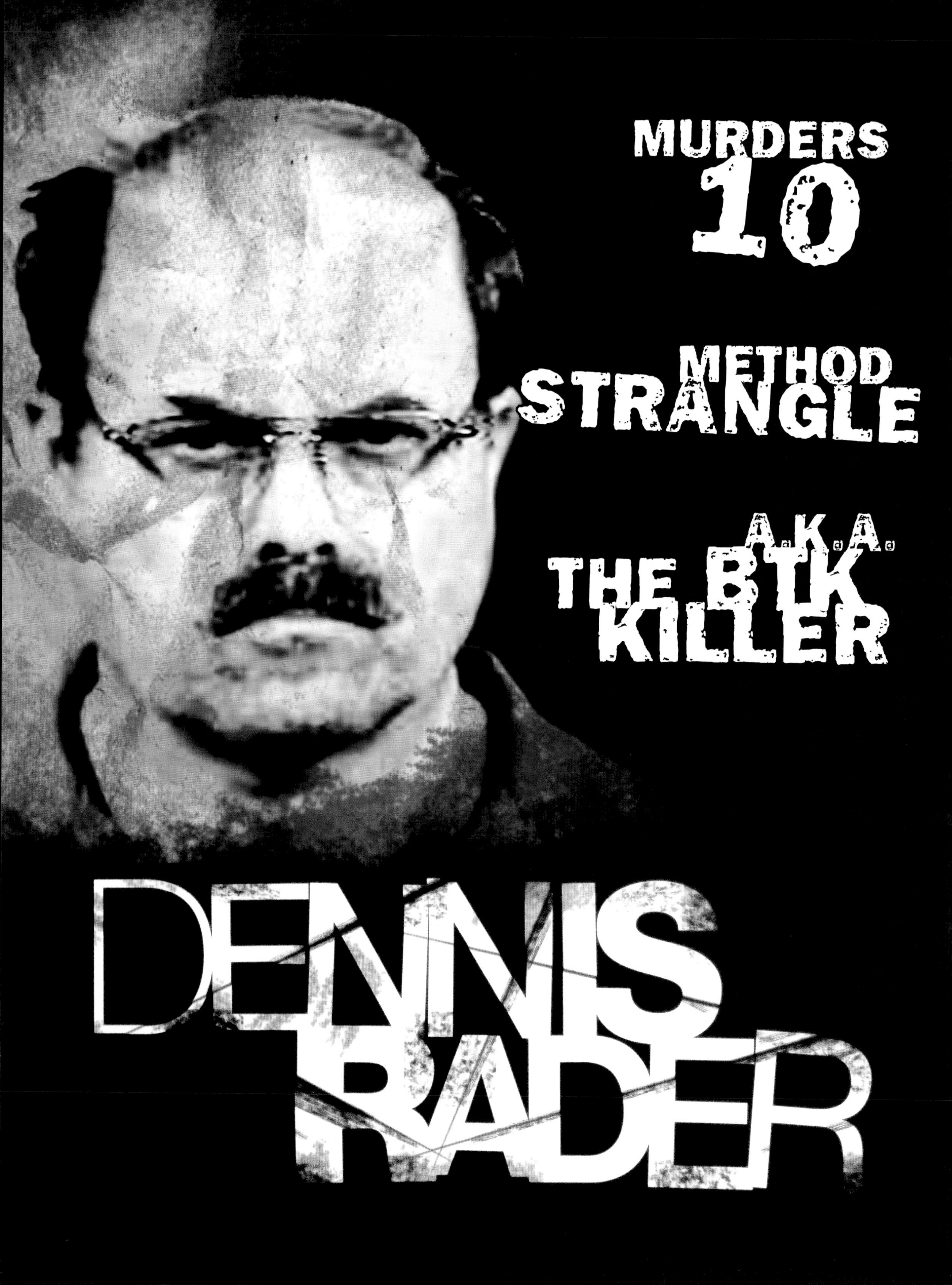

MURDERS
10

METHOD
STRANGLE

A.K.A.
THE BTK
KILLER

DENNIS
RADER

Dennis Rader was better known as the **BTK killer** – the moniker stood for **bind** them – **torture** them – **kill** them. Like the Zodiac, he was a **publicity hungry**, media savvy serial killer who would stop at nothing to attract the **attention he so craved**.

*The Wichita Eagle*, the largest circulation newspaper in the city, received a letter from a man calling himself Bill Thomas Killman, in March 2004. The writer claimed to have killed Vicki Wegerle in September 1988, saying she was a victim of the BTK Killer, the name adopted by a man who was already known to have killed seven people in Wichita from 1974 to 1978. The killer gave himself the name after his modus operandi – bind, torture, kill. At the time of the killings he sent numerous letters to the police and news media in Wichita, but this was the first communication for 25 years. It included a photocopy of Vicki Wegerle's driving licence, known to have been taken from the scene of her murder.

Over the following year the BTK Killer sent letters and packages to newspapers and TV stations in Wichita on a regular basis and left cereal packets with items taken from other victims in places where they could easily be found. He claimed to have killed a total of ten people, including Vicki Wegerle and two other women whose murders had not previously been attributed to him. In one letter he asked the police if they could trace a computer disc back to him if he sent one to them. They placed an advert in *The Wichita Eagle* saying they couldn't and, on 16 February 2005, a disc arrived at the offices of the Wichita TV station KSAS. Needless to say, the police had not been completely honest with the killer. Forensic computer specialists traced the disc to a surprising source – the Lutheran Church in Wichita. They also got the username of Dennis from the disc. The president of the Wichita Lutheran Church Council was Dennis Rader.

The first of the murders took place on 15 January 1974. On coming back home from school fifteen-year-old Charlie Otero found the bodies of his mother and father in their bedroom. Both had been strangled with what turned out to be the cord from a venetian blind. He tried to phone the police, but the line had been cut. A neighbour made the call and, when the police arrived, they found the bodies of nine-year-old Joseph Otero and his eleven-year-old sister Josephine. Joseph had also been strangled and Josephine was found hanging by the neck from a pipe in the basement. None of the victims had been sexually assaulted, but the police found semen on some of their bodies. It looked like the killer masturbated on them after he killed them.

Three months later, on 4 April, the same man cut the phone lines of the house where Kathryn Bright, and her brother Kevin lived, and he broke in while they were not there. When they got home he tied them both to chairs at gunpoint and attempted to strangle them, without killing either. Before leaving he stabbed Kathryn Bright three times in the stomach. She died later that day in hospital.

In December 1974 a man phoned The Wichita Eagle to say there was a letter about the murders hidden in a particular book on the shelves of the Wichita Public Library. The letter contained details of the crimes the police had not made public and the writer promised that there would be more killings. It also used the BTK name. He sent a number of other letters, but it was three years before the BTK Killer struck again. In 1977 two women, Shirley Vian and Nancy Fox were killed in two separate attacks. The BTK Killer cut the phone lines and broke into their houses while they were out. He appeared to know their movements during the day and had probably watched them for some time before attacking them. When the women got home, he strangled them and masturbated over their bodies. The police found the killer had taken some of their possessions, but nothing of any real value. He appeared to be taking them as mementos of his

FORENSIC COMPUTER SPECIALISTS TRACED THE DISC TO A SURPRISING SOURCE – THE LUTHERAN CHURCH IN WICHITA.

crimes. The BTK Killer began writing to newspapers and TV stations in Wichita again, asking them how many people he had to kill before they put his name on the front page.

The two killings caused panic in Wichita. People began checking to see if their phone lines had been cut every time they entered their houses. On 28 April 1979 the BTK Killer broke into 63-year-old Kathy Page-Hauptman's house. He waited for her to show up and, when she didn't, got tired of waiting and left. A few days later he wrote to her, sending her a scarf he had stolen from her house and saying 'Be glad you weren't here, because I was.'

After that the BTK Killer stopped writing letters. The investigation into the murders gradually wound down, although the file was never closed completely, until the BTK Killer resurfaced in 2004. When Dennis Rader's name first came up after being connected with the disc from the Lutheran Church, he appeared an unlikely suspect. As well as being a regular churchgoer, he had been married for more than 30 years and had two grown up children. He had served with the US Air Force and, after leaving, taken a degree at Wichita State University. From 1974 to 1988, the period when most of the murders were committed, Rader worked for ADT Security Services in Wichita, where he, no doubt, learned how to break into houses without setting off the alarms. After leaving ADT he worked for the council of Park City, the suburb of Wichita where he lived, in the Compliance Department. He was considered a conscientious worker, although a few people complained he was over zealous.

Before arresting Rader, the police took a tissue sample from his daughter and compared her DNA to samples of semen recovered from the BTK murder scenes. It gave a positive match for Dennis Rader. On 25 February 2005 Rader

was arrested. At first he maintained his innocence, but in June 2005 he pleaded guilty to ten charges of murder. He was sentenced to ten consecutive life sentences, totalling 175 years in prison, without the possibility of parole. It was the harshest sentence the trial judge could hand down. On being asked why he had broken his silence after 25 years, Rader said he was bored now that his children were grown up and didn't have anything else to do.

BTK Killer Dennis Rader begins his life sentence at the El Dorado Correctional Facility on 19 August, 2005.

MURDERS
**12+**

METHOD
**BLUDGEON**

EXECUTION
**LETHAL
INJECTION**

ÁNGEL
RESENDIZ

**Angel Reséndiz was anything but angelic.** He used the train network of North America to travel the length and breadth of the US, carrying out **frenzied attacks** on anyone and everyone who got in his way. His sister attempted to get him help by brokering a deal with the police but it was a trap, and Résendiz would **die by lethal injection** at the hands of the Texan authorities.

Dr Claudia Benton, who was 39 years old, lived with her husband and their twin daughters in a house backing on to a branch of the Union Pacific Railroad in West University Place, a neighbourhood on the edge of Houston, Texas. On 17 December 1998 she drove home from the Baylor College of Medicine, where she worked, and, as soon as she stepped in through the front door of her house, was attacked by an intruder. The man raped and stabbed her and then bludgeoned her to death with a brass statue he had found in the house. He took anything he could find of value from Dr Benton's house and drove away in her Jeep Cherokee. It was found abandoned a few days later in San Antonio, Texas, not far from the Mexican border. The police recovered a set of fingerprints

from the steering wheel which matched those of Ángel Maturino Reséndiz, a 39-year-old illegal immigrant from Mexico.

At the time, Reséndiz was known to the police in a number of states. He first came to their attention in 1976 after being arrested while illegally crossing the Mexican border into Brownsville, Texas. After two months he was deported back to Mexico, but, from then on, he constantly crossed back and forth across the border. Reséndiz was always on the move while he was in America, travelling as a hobo on freight trains and committing crimes wherever he went

In September 1979 he was arrested for car theft and assault in Miami, Florida, and was sentenced to 20 years in prison. He was released on parole after six years and repatriated to Mexico. Over the course of the next 20 years he was arrested in Texas, Louisiana, Missouri and New Mexico for a range of different petty crimes and under a variety of different names.

Although it would only emerge later, Reséndiz had already killed at least twice by the time of the attack on Dr Benton. On 29 August 1997 he attacked two University of Kentucky students as they were walking along railway lines near Lexington. Christopher Maier was bludgeoned to death with a rock and his girlfriend, Holly Dunn, was raped and severely beaten, although she would survive the attack. The second attack came more than a year later, on 4 October 1998. Reséndiz broke into the home of 87-year-old Leafie Mason via a window. The front door of Mason's house, in Hughes Springs, Texas, was no more than 50 yards from the Kansas City Southern Rail Line railway tracks. Reséndiz beat the old lady to death with a tire iron and stole everything he could carry.

Late at night on 4 May 1999, five months after the murder of Dr Benton, Reséndiz broke into the parsonage of the United Church of Christ, which was adjacent to the railway tracks in Weimar, Texas. He attacked Norman Sirnic, 46, the pastor of the church, and his wife Karen, 47, while they were sleeping. Both were battered to death with a sledgehammer. Their car was found in San Antonio three weeks later. Fingerprints connected the murders with the earlier attack on Dr Benton.

Two separate attacks on people living near the railway lines in Texas occurred in one day, 4 June 1999. Noemi Dominguez, 26, a schoolteacher in Houston, was clubbed to death in her apartment. Her car was found a week later near the bridge over the Rio Grande, which marks the Mexican border, in Del Rio, Texas. That night Josephine Konvicka, 73, was attacked in her home in Fayette County, Texas, not far from Weimar. She was killed by a single blow to the head from a pickaxe as she was sleeping in her bed. DNA from Noemi Dominguez was found in Konvicka's house, leading the police to suppose that Reséndiz drove to Konvicka's house after killing Dominguez.

# RESENDIZ TRAVELLED THROUGH THE STATES CONSTANTLY, GOING WHEREVER THE FIRST FREIGHT TRAIN HE COULD HOP ONTO WOULD TAKE HIM

By now it was obvious a serial killer was targeting people who lived near railway tracks and then heading for Mexico. Although many of the victims were women and some had been raped, the police considered the primary motivation was money. The suspect was known to be an alcoholic and habitual drug user and, they thought, was committing crimes mainly to feed his habits. After being identified from his fingerprints, Reséndiz initially appeared on the FBI's Ten Most Wanted list as Rafael Ramirez, one of at least 30 different aliases he is thought to have used. The problem faced by the FBI was that Reséndiz travelled through the United States constantly, going wherever the first freight train he could hop would take him. He travelled from Florida to California and from Mexico as far north as Canada. The FBI and other law enforcement agencies knew who he was and what he looked like, but he lived in an underworld of hobos and illegal immigrants, putting him beyond the reach of the law.

Reséndiz struck again on 15 June. He shot 80-year-old George Morbor in the head with a shotgun and beat his 52-year-old daughter Carolyn Frederick to death with the stock of the gun after he had broken into their mobile home near the railway tracks in Gorham, Illinois. The following day Frederick's red pickup truck was seen in Cairo, Illinois, 96 km (60 miles) away, being driven by a man who matched Reséndiz's description. By this time panic had struck the areas of Texas and Illinois where the murders had been committed, particularly among those people who lived near railway lines. The mayor of Weimar, where three people had been killed, explained to a journalist who asked him how people in the town were feeling that all the stores in the area had sold out of guns.

By this time, Texas Ranger Drew Carter had made contact with Reséndiz's sister, Manuela, who lived in Albuquerque,

New Mexico, and asked her to help the investigation. She thought Reséndiz would either be killed by the FBI or would kill again himself and she agreed to try and persuade him to surrender. She contacted him through a relative who lived in Ciudad Juarez, just over the Mexican border from El Paso, which was where Reséndiz was thought to be hiding out. The FBI and district attorney's office in Harris County, Texas, jointly offered Reséndiz a deal. If he surrendered they would guarantee his safety in jail, allow his mother, sister

OPPOSITE PAGE: Weimar United Church of Christ, where Norman Sirnic was pastor.
BELOW: Ángel Maturino Reséndiz points at Texas Ranger Sgt. Drew Carter accusing him of lying under oath after being sentenced to death by lethal injection on Monday 22 May 2000 in Houston.

and wife to visit him and he would be given a psychological evaluation before he was put on trial. Reséndiz sent a message to his sister to say he agreed to the terms. On 13 July he met Drew Carter on the bridge connecting Ciudad Juarez with El Paso. They shook hands and Carter took Reséndiz into custody.

Unless there was a part of the deal that has not been made public, it is not entirely clear why Reséndiz accepted the terms. No promises were made about the type of sentence he could expect at his trial. Texas has the highest rate of invoking the death penalty

BELOW: George Benton, husband of murder victim Claudia Benton, makes a statement to the press following the execution of Ángel Reséndiz by lethal injection.

for murder of any state in America. Reséndiz must have known what he was likely to face if he was put on trial there. Had he surrendered in Mexico, he would not have been extradited to America. Mexico has a policy of not sending prisoners back to countries where they might face the death penalty. There have been suggestions that Reséndiz had become the target of numerous bounty hunters, who wanted to claim the $125,000 reward for his capture. Reséndiz may have thought the bounty hunters intended to kill him rather than take him alive. There is also the possibility that he had committed murders in Mexico and, thinking he would be caught by the Mexican police if he stayed there, preferred to take his chances in the American justice system. There have been a huge number of women murdered in Ciudad Juarez over the past 20 years, some estimates putting the figure at over 400. Reséndiz could have been responsible for some of these murders, although, as they have continued after he surrendered, certainly not all of them.

Reséndiz was put on trial in Harris County, Texas, on 8 May 2000. Although known to have killed nine people at this point, the trial only concerned the murder of Dr Claudia Benton. The evidence against Reséndiz for this killing was compelling. He was linked to the crime scene by DNA analysis and his fingerprints were found in Dr Benton's jeep. Items stolen from Dr Benton's house were found in the possession of Julietta Reyes, Reséndiz's common-law wife in Mexico. The defence, recognizing the overwhelming evidence against Reséndiz, attempted to present him to the jury as being insane. The prosecution called expert witnesses, who comprehensively showed that Reséndiz was well aware of the consequences of his actions at the time of the murder. The jury found him guilty and he was sentenced to death.

While on Death Row, Reséndiz admitted to a further three murders in the US, bringing the total he is known to have committed to 12. The FBI think he could have been involved in a number of other unsolved murders which occurred near railway tracks in other parts of America and bear all the hallmarks of Reséndiz's modus operandi. The Mexican authorities also have a number of similar cases. Although it would be a little too convenient for law enforcement agencies to clear some murders off their books by pinning them on Reséndiz, there can be little doubt he was responsible for more deaths than those to which he confessed.

The appeals process lasted for six years. After it had failed, on 21 June 2006, Reséndiz was judged mentally fit to be executed. Not all of the psychiatrists who spoke to Reséndiz agreed with the decision. Some considered him to be delusional and borderline schizophrenic. Despite these reservations, the sentence was carried out on 27 June by lethal injection. George Benton, Dr Claudia Benton's husband, was present at the execution and said afterwards that Reséndiz was 'evil contained in human form, a creature without a soul, no conscience, no sense of remorse, no regard for the sanctity of human life'.

## THE APPEALS PROCESS LASTED FOR SIX YEARS. AFTER IT HAD FAILED, ON 21 JUNE 2006, RESÉNDIZ WAS JUDGED MENTALLY FIT TO BE EXECUTED

BELOW: Members of the Texas Death Penalty Abolition Movement protest outside the Walls Unit prior to the execution of Ángel Reséndiz

# INDEX

This index does not contain the names of any victims, see individual articles for full details.